Ignite Your
Enthusiasm
and Make
Your Dreams
Come True

ARE YOU FIRED UP?

Anne Whiting

Are You Fired Up?

Anne Whiting

Published by
Possibility Press
e-mail: PossPress@aol.com

Manufactured in the United States of America

Dedication

To my loving husband, Spencer.

Acknowledgments

I am grateful for all the help I've received from so many people who helped make this book possible. You know who you are. Thank you so much.

Are You Fired Up?
—An Acronym For Success

Aim high and dream.

Rekindle yourself by writing down your dreams.

Expect yourself to keep dreaming bigger.

You need to get help from people who are where you want to be.

Organize and energize yourself by sharing your dream with your mentor or leader.

Use goal setting to take charge of your life.

Fire up your life by working toward your dreams.

Ignite your dreams by dreambuilding.

Request career and business-building counseling from your leader or mentor to—*get on the fast track of success.*

Enthusiastically follow the system of success for your industry.

Dreams *do* come true, when you get *fired up* and consistently take action—*never giving up.*

Use every career and business-building tool you can, and attend every seminar recommended by your leader or mentor.

Pursue your dream and help others pursue theirs—*with passion, persistence, and a positive vision of the outcome.*

Contents

Introduction

"If you can dream it, you can do it."
Walt Disney

Whatever Happened to Your Dreams?

As a child, did you ever dream *big* dreams? Were you excited about life? Did you believe you were really going to make a difference in the world? What happened when you grew up? Did you keep your dreams alive or did you let someone "steal" your dreams? Are you fired up about life, and making your dreams come true?

Inside you are all the talents you need to make your dreams come true. You have unique gifts to share with the world and only *you* can offer them. There's only one you!

Little children have great big dreams which seem totally attainable when they are young, open-minded, full of wonder and idealistic. For most young children, the sky's the limit. But sometimes their fire and enthusiasm gets doused, or at least dampened, by negative thinking role models and the challenges of growing up. If that happens, dreams are often forgotten. The child becomes an adult who, in most cases, leads a day to day existence, just "getting by."

Challenges Can Be Our Teachers

Many people live, day to day, with a sense of resignation believing they have to take whatever life dishes out. This is just not true. Then there are people who wait until they experience a major challenge before they stop and look at their lives. All of a sudden, they "wake up" and realize something's missing. They're bored with the same old routine and want more meaning and happiness in their lives.

But rest assured you can create the life you want, whether your goals and dreams are big or small.

Through an extremely challenging childhood, I experienced crisis after crisis. My mother became seriously ill when I was six; she was in and out of the hospital for the next fifteen years until she finally died. Alcoholism was a constant presence in the family, and like most children from that environment, I grew up insecure and scared. When I was in my late twenties, I nearly married an alcoholic. Fortunately, I learned a lot from those experiences. I got the help I needed through therapy, personal growth workshops and recovery support groups, and became a stronger adult as a result.

As I learned and grew, I was able to break free of the past. I know now that those crises were blessings in disguise, for they taught me compassion and understanding, strength and courage, perseverance and faith. With the support of others, I have been triumphant in overcoming the negativity and stepping forward into my dreams. My dreams helped keep me going, and they remain an essential part of my life.

As a child, my dreams were to be a teacher, help other people, and be happily married. As I grew older, I wanted to do even more, from opening my own business to writing books. Through it all, my dreams have helped sustain me.

Have there been times in your life when you have broken free from the bonds of the past and succeeded, even when it seemed nearly impossible? Many people have such experiences during athletic events, where they're able to set new records or exceed their personal best. Do you remember what it was like the first time you helped someone with a challenge? It felt great, right? Did you ever throw a surprise birthday party for someone you love? These are examples of being fired up about life. And when you're fired up exciting things can happen.

So What about Your Dreams?

How about those dreams you had when you were a child? Are you living them? Do you still want them? Or, do you now have other dreams that are equally or more important to you, but maybe you're not quite sure where to start?

Don't worry. You *can* make your dreams come true and start living a more fulfilling and satisfying life. Many of the answers about how you can do that are in this book

Making a Difference in the World

You can also make a difference in the world—big or small. You are a unique person who can touch the lives of others in a special way. In fact, you're already making a difference in ways you may be unaware of.

As a speaker and trainer, I have seen amazing results when people strive for their dreams. When people believe in themselves, get fired up and start taking action on their dreams, miracles can happen. I have witnessed case after case of people overcoming obstacles, going for their dreams and succeeding against all odds.

That can happen for you, too. You have the power and ability to make your dreams come true. You may have the most splendid dreams. But, they'll just remain "Someday I'll…" wishes unless you get fired up and focus on making them a reality.

The Birth of *Are You Fired Up?*

I love watching people move on their dreams—it's so inspiring. Everyone is like a match lighting kindling. The fire inside of me was set ablaze. I learned that my deepest fulfillment comes from helping others take action on their dreams and make them come true.

Through the years, I have discovered that, while almost everyone has a dream, very few people actually *experience* their dreams. Since there is no training for it in school, most people don't know *how* to make their dreams come true, *how* to take action or *how* to follow through and succeed. So many of them die "with their music still in them." But it doesn't have to be that way.

You have an excellent opportunity to realize your goals and dreams. Associate with fine role models who have already blazed the path before you. To be successful, enthusiastically follow your dream, letting *no* obstacle stand in your way. Follow your dream and it will take you where you need to go as long as you are fired up and take action.

When you are fired up great things happen—even miracles. You can achieve more than you may now think is possible. I hope this book helps you get fired up about your life and helps you overcome obstacles you may have let stop you in the past. It has tools, techniques and real-life stories of ordinary people just like you and me who overcame their challenges and made their dreams come true. Their experiences are shared to inspire and support you in achieving *your* dreams.

If you've been looking for ways to have more success, happiness, love and wealth in your life, continue reading. Maybe your dream is to be financially free so you can spend more time with your family, traveling and doing other things you love to do.

Your future begins today. You *can* do whatever it takes to do what you love and live your dream. It's just a decision away.

I appreciate the lessons God has taught me in the creation of this book. And I hope it will help you on your quest to be more fired up.

The Fire Inside You

Inside of you is the fire of life. That fire is your passion, your life purpose, your mission and your fulfillment. It ignites and burns brightly inside of you when you are doing whatever it takes to live your dreams. When you're fired up your fire warms others, igniting their flames and creating excitement and a desire to join you so they can make their dreams come true, too.

When you're fired up you feel strong, vibrantly alive and courageous. You believe you can overcome any obstacle and meet any challenge head-on and win. You believe you can achieve what may have seemed unthinkable to you in the past.

You *can* have more happiness and success than you ever imagined. It all starts inside of you—with your fire and your dreams. The choice is always ours. The time to live the life of your dreams is now. As Goethe once said, *"Whatever you can do, or dream you can, begin it. Boldness has genius, power and magic in it. Begin it now."*

Are you fired up? Then let's get started.

With love to you all,

Anne

The *Are You Fired Up?* Principles

#1 Choose and Commit to Success
#2 Dreambuild Often
#3 Doing What You Love To Do Makes A Difference in the World Around You
#4 Get Absolutely Clear About What You *Really, Really* Want
#5 Use Your Imagination
#6 Uncover Your Myths
#7 Identify Role Models
#8 Listen to Motivational Tapes and Attend Seminars
#9 Act "As If"
#10 Take action and Keep Moving
#11 Have A Plan
#12 Capture Your Creativity on Paper
#13 Use Your Resources
#14 Connect With The Right People
#15 Manage Your Money and Get Out of Debt
#16 Remain Unattached to Outcomes
#17 Be Patient
#18 Use Your Time Wisely
#19 Take Care of Your Health
#20 Laugh About It
#21 Dreams Help Keep You Alive
#22 It Could Happen
#23 Learn From Your Mistakes
#24 Cultivate an Attitude of Gratitude
#25 Use Affirmations
#26 Use Action Options to Get Fired Up
#27 Finish What You Start
#28 Create a Dream Collage
#29 Let the Little Child Inside You Heart Come Out and Play
#30 Avoid the Hooks
#31 Do What Winners Do to Stay Fired Up
#32 Make a Difference!

Chapter 1

Your Dreams Create Your Life

Your Belief Is Your Fuel

"Nothing happens unless first a dream."
Carl Sandburg

There's a Fire Inside You

There is nobody else just like you, and you uniquely reflect your enthusiasm to the world when you are fired up about your life. You have the ability to touch the lives of others and live a life of happiness and success. Whatever you have or haven't done up until now is in the past. The rest of your life begins today, right now, in the present moment. And the *present* is a gift you give yourself.

Dreams keep the fires inside you alive. As you anticipate and develop your dreams and make them come true, your life takes on new meaning and value. You enjoy greater success and you feel more in control and excited about your life. You are also more attractive to others.

When you do whatever it takes to do what you love to do, and enjoy the journey as well as the results, your enthusiasm shows and automatically uplifts others. It's contagious, and can spark other people into action. The fire ignites and spreads from you to others. Your dreams then start coming true, one after another, as you help others reach their goals.

We've all had experiences when we've been fired up or we've seen someone else who was fired up. Olympic speed skater Dan Jansen at the 1994 Winter Olympics is one example. People were excited that he finally won after all his disappointing losses. He persevered and triumphed! He won the gold medal and demonstrated that, with persistence and a positive attitude, you can make your dreams come true.

Perhaps you've seen the movie *Dances With Wolves*, which portrays how the United States military uprooted Native Americans from their homes, treating them like animals. Kevin Costner directed and produced this movie, against all odds, with very little support from Hollywood. A masterpiece that stirred the hearts of those who watched it, that film went on to receive great acclaim. It brought in millions of dollars at the box office and was culturally recognized as authentic by many Native Americans. He pursued his dream with passion and excellence, producing a movie that reflected his enthusiasm. As people watched the film, they got fired up too.

Jansen and Costner are but two examples of people who were fired up about their lives and went on to achieve their dreams. You, too, can have exciting experiences. You can make your dreams come true, step by step. You can be passionate about life, working towards your dreams and doing more of what you love as they come true.

Why Aren't More People *Fired Up?*
If it's true that every one of us has a fire inside, as well as unique gifts and talents, why aren't more people living the lives they've dreamed about? Part of the answer is the lack of a positive, proactive education.

I taught English and history to junior high students (ages 13-16) in the mid-1970's. I saw many youngsters negatively labeled, as they were placed in classes according to their "intelligence." While teaching English to a class of "low level academic" boys in the ninth grade, I saw firsthand how destructive labels are. Those boys didn't believe in themselves and thought they were failures.

When I spoke to them the first day, I did my best to "wipe their mental slates clean." I told them that every student in the class could make an A, *if they worked for it.* Most of them didn't trust me—at first. Then, as we spent more time together, they understood that I really did believe in them and was willing to work with them to help them learn.

Little by little, small miracles occurred. One boy, who hated reading, began regularly volunteering to read aloud to the class. Two others immediately saw their work pay off in the form of Bs on the first test. They were stunned. By the end of the year, there were many Bs, several Cs and only one D. No one failed that class!

Besides discovering they could read, write and communicate effectively, these boys learned they were intelligent and capable, even though labeled otherwise. Up until that time, they had not had that experience. They had believed their label and their behavior reflected it. They needed someone to encourage them to achieve, like we all do.

That happens to many people. Sometimes they allow negative self talk and childhood experiences to stop them from growing. They may have had negative experiences where they were labeled as failures and, as a result, gave up on themselves. Most schooling does not teach how to do whatever it takes, persistently, step by step, until you create the life you truly want, doing what you believe you are meant to do.

That's exactly what this book is all about. It's a step by step handbook for defining your dreams and becoming and staying enthusiastic as you move forward to achieve them.

You can use these ideas to accomplish any goal, dream or mission. They have been used effectively by thousands to create the lives they've always wanted. As we go along, I'll continue to share true stories, so you'll know you can do it too—become fired up and make your dreams come true.

Did You Know?

When Henry Ford wanted to produce the V-8 engine with a single block, he was told repeatedly that it was impossible. He sent his staff back to work and told them to stay on the job until they did what he asked. After a year, there was *still* no success. So, he told them to keep at it! He *knew* his determination would pay off. Eventually they did it and the V-8 became a huge success. It helped Ford and his motor company outstrip the competition and take the lead in the automotive market. He refused to believe "It's impossible."

Amy Grant, the singer and popular Grammy award winner, has multiple platinum albums. However, she launched her recording career with a big failure. While on her first tour, she was due to sign autographs and sing for an hour at a record store in southern California. Twelve hundred invitations had gone out and everyone was expecting a huge crowd. *No one showed up*—not even one person came, out of *twelve hundred* invited!

Although she seriously considered quitting music at that point, she still persevered. And look where she is today. One lesson, she learned for sure, from her rocky start, is to always appreciate her fans and *never* to take them for granted.

How it Feels to Be *Fired Up!*

Don Shula, famous football coach and author, describes what it feels like for him to be fired up. He writes, "You want to know what motivates me? When the stadium's full, the crowd is yelling and the referee raises his hand to signal the start of the game, I can feel adrenaline rush through my body. I wouldn't want to be anywhere else in the world."

That attitude led Don to break George Hala's all-time coaching record of 324 wins.

Bonnie Blair, Olympic speed skater and five-time gold medalist, is a great example of someone who is completely fired up about her life and her dream. Each time she was interviewed on television during the 1994 Olympics, she enthusiastically exclaimed, "I love to skate!"

There's nothing quite like the energy and excitement of being fired up. I actively strive to live more and more of my life fired up. It doesn't take much to make it happen. One heartfelt talk with someone can spark my enthusiasm.

I also get excited when I picture myself helping others achieve their dreams. Remembering the times when I triumphed over obstacles to reach a special goal, fills my heart with courage and the strength to keep going. Do whatever it takes to get fired up. The flame inside of you is ready to ignite. Light your fire today and start living your dreams.

Now Take These *Are You Fired Up?* Action Steps

♦ Pay attention to the other people in your life and what fires them up. Notice what excites them and let yourself get fired up by their positive energy.

♦ Review your life and recall the times when you were truly fired up. Maybe it was before a school athletic competition, a music recital or business success.

♦ Perhaps you worked all summer to earn the money to buy a car. Maybe you took a life-saving course and survived "rescuing" a kicking, screaming 200-pound "victim" struggling with you in the water. Perhaps you ran for office in a school election or acted out a major role in a school play. Whatever the events were, picture them as clearly as possible, feel the triumph and satisfaction that you had at the time. Start becoming more and more familiar with the excitement of being fired up.

Chapter 2

Negative Self Talk Can Douse Your Fire

Keeping the Embers Alive

"...your own resolution to succeed is more important than any other one thing."
Abraham Lincoln

Negative Self Talk Is a Dreamstealer

Did you know that we have between 40,000 and 50,000 thoughts a day. Alarmingly, research has shown that 75-85 percent of those thoughts are negative in most people. That's why becoming aware of negative self talk is so important.

Two reasons why more people are not living their dream is that they allow negative self talk and limiting beliefs to stop them from taking the appropriate actions. Here are some examples of people who let negative self talk steal their dream:

Mary Lets Negativity Rule

Mary sees an ad in the paper for the job she's always wanted. Instead of going after it and sharing her dynamism and excellent work skills with the people at that company, she doesn't even bother applying for the job. Why? She thinks people need to have a college degree to do that kind of job; all she has is experience. She undermines herself with negative self talk and quits before she starts. She gives up on her dream and feels discouraged.

Tom's Misperceptions Get in the Way

Tom reads a story about a local community center that needs volunteers to work with troubled youth. He's excited because he remembers how much an older man helped him when he was a struggling adolescent. But before he even meets anyone at the center, he lets his negative self talk take over.

Perceiving that he doesn't have enough training in child psychology, he fears he won't know how to handle every kind of problem he'd encounter. He also thinks he needs to be earning lots of money to be a good role model. Then his wife tells him that those kids might be dangerous, and he considers that possibility. The result is he doesn't take action; he allows his doubts and fears to keep him stuck. He ends up feeling empty and unfulfilled.

Doubt Steals Jim and Linda's Dream

Jim and Linda's life is one of mundane survival. They were given an opportunity to generate some additional income. They had a chance to take advantage of a system of continuing education—books, tapes and seminars. They know they're in a rut, yet they continue to let their fear of the unknown stop them.

They cover up their fear by using the excuse that they don't have time. They remain frustrated and bored but aren't doing anything to change their circumstances. They don't seem to understand that, as someone once said, *"Insanity is doing the same things while expecting different results."*

Just in these three examples, it's evident how strong a hold negativity can have. Even though these people have let their false beliefs stop them, that doesn't mean you need to let yours stop you. With your enthusiasm, passion, talents, and a willingness to go forward, you can make your dreams come true. Right now, at this very moment, you can start making changes in your life and begin doing whatever it takes to do more of what you love. You'll find that what you love to do reflects your innermost desires. Once you know that, you can start evaluating where you are and where you want to be. You'll start getting more and more fired up about your life.

As you begin taking steps toward living the life you've always wanted, you'll discover that you can give up the grind of something you don't enjoy—sooner than you might have thought. You may want to move on from your job or change your life in other exciting ways.

However, you'll need to have your financial situation in order before you do so. The best way to make that happen is to take action and prepare yourself for your new life. Do your homework, lay the foundation and "stack the deck" in your favor. Part of that is counseling with a mentor—someone you respect who has done what you want to do. You deserve it and you can have it—when you get fired up and make it happen!

Perhaps these stories reminded you of somebody you know. Do they sound familiar? Later, you'll learn more about the doubts and fears that people allow to stop them from having the kind of life they would like to have. Everyone has some kind of negative voice that tries to hold them back. Replace that voice with positive self talk and *take action anyway,* no matter what the negative voice says. Feel your fear and go for your dream in spite of it. When you make the decision and start taking action, amazing things can happen in extraordinary ways. Here are a few examples:

Walt Disney

Walt Disney went bankrupt several times before he achieved success. His dream of what was possible kept him going. He never quit, not ever. Now his creations, cartoons, movies and theme parks touch millions of lives every year. As he once said, *"All of our dreams can come true (when) we have the courage to pursue them."*

Abraham Lincoln

Abraham Lincoln experienced many defeats before he became one of the United States' greatest Presidents. Born poor, he lost his job, failed in business twice and failed to get elected in eight campaigns before becoming a senator. He went bankrupt and later had a nervous breakdown. He never quit; he persisted in following his dreams.

What would the U.S. be like if he had allowed his lack of formal childhood education and political success stop him from running for President? As Lincoln once said, *"...your own resolution to succeed is more important than any other one thing."*

Michael Worsley

After Michael Worsley relocated to Manchester, New Hampshire, he discovered he was one of only a few black males in the area. Instead of dwelling on the isolation and developing a negative attitude, he put his skills to use. He channeled his energies into the Webster House, where he nurtures neglected children from broken homes with self-esteem, love and encouragement. He regularly receives feedback from area professionals about the positive impact of his work on these children. He makes a big difference in their lives, which, in turn, affects their behavior with others.

Is Fire and Enthusiasm Enough?

Success takes much more than fire and enthusiasm—*it takes commitment, determination, focus, planning, personal development, clarity and consistent action.* It also starts with having a strong desire—a dream. You need to know what you have let get in the way until now and what you need to do to be more successful. The more information you have about your dream—what motivates you to keep going—the more likely you are to achieve it.

The more you are aware of your false beliefs and negative self talk, the sooner the better. Let them go and replace them with new beliefs and behaviors which support your dream.

The more you use the ideas in this book as well as continually educating yourself about your field of endeavor, the sooner you can be living your dream. Once you achieve your first dream, you can use the same pattern of success over and over again to achieve your other dreams.

You can even use it to make your current dream even bigger. You can be doing the things you love to do, and consistently experience greater success, fulfillment, wealth, and happiness.

Are You Fired Up? **Principle #1—***Choose and Commit to Success*

Did you know that choice and commitment are very powerful? Every great achievement came as a result of choice and commitment. Olympic athletes *choose* to spend hours and hours every day training for an event that comes once every four years. After they have made the choice and committed to it, their actions and attitudes naturally fall into line.

When you make the choice to personally develop yourself and commit to it, you are saying yes to your future. You are actively setting into motion a *willingness* to succeed and an openness to opportunity and good fortune. You are instilling the attitude of doing whatever it takes.

You are freeing up your thinking to help you achieve your dream. Such choice and commitment are deliberate and intentional; they clarify your direction and help you stay focused as you take action.

To win or lose,
To love or hate,
To strive or quit,
To risk or withdraw,
To accelerate or hesitate,
To dream or stagnate,
To open or close,
To succeed or fail,
To live or die.
Everyone of these
starts with a
CHOICE.

So What About Your Dream?

The choice is yours. You can live the same life you've always lived—which may be just fine. But you're probably reading this because you want more out of life. You know, deep down inside, that *you deserve more.* Whether it's more time with your family, more money, a bigger home, freedom from your current job or conventional business, more time to have fun, traveling, a way to touch the lives of others, or to support your favorite charities, more happiness and love, or something else—*you can have it.*

To begin, all you need to do is *choose, commit,* and start taking action. Follow your dream and it'll take you where you're supposed to go. Once you know the *"why,"* you'll figure out the *"how."* It only takes a tiny spark to light a huge fire. And you have hundreds of sparks inside you. Start discovering them now and let them get you fired up. Remember the words of William James, *"To change (your) life: Start immediately. Do it flamboyantly. No exceptions."*

Now Take These *Are You Fired Up?* Action Steps

♦ Read positive inspirational, motivational, and educational books that your leader or mentor recommends.

♦ If you like uplifting movies, watch videos like *Field of Dreams* or *Rudy* to inspire you.

♦ Actively choose your success. On a 3" x 5" card, write *"I, (your name), choose and commit to succeed in life and make my dreams come true."* Carry this card with you in your wallet and look at it every day. You can also put it on your bathroom mirror or some other places where you'll see it often.

♦ If you know what your dream is, write that down too. For example— "We, John and Mary Smith, choose and commit to succeed in life and in making our dream of being financially free come true."

Chapter 3

Discovering Your Dream

Locating The Spark Inside

"People are always blaming their circumstances for what they are. I don't believe in circumstances. The people who get on in this world are the people who get up and look for the circumstances they want, and if they can't find them, make them."
George Bernard Shaw

Where Do You Begin?

Have you ever known anyone with enthusiasm and a sincere desire to change, but they didn't know where to begin or even what their dream might be? This is quite common. Many people have little or no idea how to discover their dream. They don't know how they can make their rough ideas take shape and develop into a dream they're excited about.

While many people have interest, commitment and curiosity, they often need to become clear about what they really want. So where do you start? It's really very simple. Start with what you enjoy doing. Also, what would you like to have that, perhaps, you've wanted for awhile?

Are You Fired Up? **Principle #2—*Dreambuild Often***

The people who are the happiest, consistently successful and fired up about their lives, always keep their dream in front of them. They make it come true by regularly focusing on it and consistently taking action to make it happen. Drive your dream vehicle and walk through your dream home. Take pictures and take home some brochures. Look at these things often. Stay in touch with your dream constantly, so you know why you're building your business or profession. Take your spouse dreambuilding with you.

Peter Loves Giving Presentations and Sharing His Opportunity, Products and Services With Others

Peter works from home, building his own independent business. Watching him in action when he meets with prospects, associates and clients is exciting. He's fired up because he knows he is sharing something of value with people. The caring he has for people shows in the way he listens and asks questions. His excitement about what he is doing is obvious. His eyes light up as he realizes he can help people overcome obstacles and grow. It's obvious he loves working with people and helping them. He is fired up when he shares with others as he builds his future.

Sharing and Listening Builds Dreams

Often the best way to understand something is to experience it. To know the feeling of being fired up that comes from talking about what you love to do, you may want to do this next brief activity. It'll also give you the opportunity to practice effective listening. It only takes six minutes and it's a lot of fun. All you'll need is somebody who can sit with you for a few minutes, plus a stopwatch, clock or timer. Pick someone, like your spouse, who is supportive of you and what you do.

Set a timer for three minutes. Sit down and take turns playing the roles of sharer and listener. The sharer talks for three minutes about what they love to do. They go into detail about each activity, describing specifically what they love about it, and they keep talking until the time is up. If there are periods of silence, that's fine. The role of the listener is to actively listen; that means giving full attention to the sharer and not saying a word; just listening during those three minutes, even if there is silence. The listener is to have consistent eye contact with the sharer—giving their full attention to that person, observing their level of enthusiasm and the twinkle in their eyes.

Author M. Scott Peck, in *The Road Less Traveled*, says, *"True listening, total concentration on the other (person), is always a manifestation of love."* To be truly listened to is a rare experience in our world. It is a gift of great value. Savor it!

Then after three minutes, switch roles. Reset the timer. Now the first person listens attentively, silently, with total eye contact, while their "partner" shares about what *they* love to do. The listener observes the body language of their "partner" to see how animated they become. The listener looks into their eyes for the sparkle. It's often a happy experience with a lot of laughter on both sides.

After both of you have shared, talk briefly about what you've experienced. Notice how you feel and what your voice sounds like. Most people become highly energized during this process, and use their hands as they talk fast and laugh a lot. It's fun to hear others share what they love to do. It's also exciting to share what you love doing.

It's invigorating to do what you enjoy doing the most. You're meant to do what you love to do, to live fully experiencing your dream and share the dream with others. You're meant to be fired up about life. When you are working on your dream, you're maximizing your ability to succeed. You're in your best state of mind to achieve goals.

Are You Fired Up? Principle #3—*Doing What You Love to Do Makes a Difference in the World Around You*

When you're doing whatever it takes to do what you love to do and live your dreams, you're automatically making a positive difference in the world! Your happiness and excitement attract and inspire others to join you. It's like striking a match to a pile of dry kindling. One ignites and sparks the next and then the next, until a blaze is burning bright.

The listening activity can help you understand yourself and others. It can assist you in fine-tuning your listening and observing skills. The most effective leaders know that the best way to create long-lasting relationships is to *be* sincerely interested in others, discover their dreams and dreambuild each time you see them. This could include doing something as simple as borrowing a travel video of their favorite dream vacation from the local travel agency and watching it together. Or it may mean going to see some beautiful houses nearby that are open for public inspection.

Eventually, your associates will know you care about them and start linking you with what they enjoy. As a result, they're more likely to have a good feeling when you're around them. This can help your relationships grow stronger and more positive, and they're likely to be more receptive to what you say. They'll understand that you have their best interests at heart.

Do Your Family and Friends Really Know You?

Family members also need to share what they love to do with each other. Do you believe your family really knows what you enjoy doing? If your family is among the small number who do freely share what they're most passionate about doing, consider yourself fortunate. Oftentimes, your family members remember you as a child. Many of them may not realize how you've grown, what sparks your enthusiasm, how much you want to succeed, and what you're capable of doing.

How many unsuitable birthday presents have you received from family members and friends you thought knew you? Do you want to develop stronger bonds with those you care about most? Find out what gets them fired up. Learn about their dreams, what they'll love to do, where they'd like to go and what they'd like to have. Make a point of asking about these things frequently—whether or not you share their interests.

Your attention will show that what matters to them, matters to you. It will help you be a better spouse, parent, sibling, son, daughter or friend. This will also make it easier for you to share ideas and opportunities with them, if you choose to do so, along the line.

Your Fire Energizes Them

Did you know that other people can sense something different about you when you are working towards your dream? It's true. You probably have a spring in your step and a sparkle in your eyes. Just like when you share what you'd love to do, your enthusiasm for life shines out from you to others.

One of the people at my bank often comments that I always sound so upbeat and positive when I talk to him on the phone. That's because I am working towards my dream. I look forward to getting up in the morning. I'm fired up.

Can you picture what the world would be like if more and more people would focus on their dreams? The U.S. statistics from Gallup polls say that nearly two-thirds of all people hate getting up and going to work. More heart attacks occur on Monday mornings before 9 a.m. than any other time.

What if these people were focused and working on making their dreams come true? What if they were energetic and excited to get out of bed to start their day? This would be a different world. It would be pretty amazing! You can start living your life that way right now. You can begin by learning about what you want the most in your life.

Are You Fired Up? **Principle #4—Get Absolutely Clear About What You Really, Really Want**

You need to know what your dream is before you can focus on it. And you probably won't know what your dream is until you look at what you want in your life. Until you know what you want with absolute certainty, you won't put your best efforts into it. It'll take much longer to make your dream come true.

Here's an activity to help you clarify what you want. On a piece of paper, make two columns like those shown in the next graphic, one on the left and one on the right. Number each from one to ten. On the left, list ten things you have in your life right now which you don't want—*your circumstances.* On the right, write down what you do want—*your dreams.*

Circumstances	Dreams
1. Debt.	1. Financial Freedom.
2. A broken down car.	2. A new car.
3. A boring job.	3. To be free of the job.

Next, draw an X through all the circumstances. Focus on and put your energy into your dreams—what you *do* want. You get what you focus on.

Ask yourself this question with each of the items in the dream column: "If I could have this right now, would I really take it?" If the answer is anything but an absolute yes, cross it off. Put your attention on what you're *sure* you want. Clarity is key. You've got to have a dream first before you can make it come true!

I personally know how well making this list works. In 1986 I did it. One dream item was "a beautiful sunny home on the water" which, at that time, I had pictured as an oceanfront villa. One night, while sitting at home, I suddenly got the idea of buying a house. I checked the Sunday paper, and sure enough, there was an ad with a headline that read "Live on the Water." I spent the entire afternoon walking around the advertised property, which sat on a riverbank. It was easy to imagine living there—it was so peaceful and lovely. The very next day, I bought the property—and soon they began building my new home. I visited the construction site every week and watched it take shape. Now my husband and I live in that beautiful sunny home on the water! You can live in *your* dream house, too. Get fired up today and start creating the life you want. Consider the words of Thomas Edison who said, *"I never worked a day in my life...it was all fun."*

Now Take These *Are You Fired Up?* Action Steps

- ◆ Take time to listen to your family and friends. Find out what they love to do and bring it up in your conversations often. Genuinely care about them and their interests.
- ◆ Next time you go to meet with a new friend, a client, or business associate, find out what they love to do for fun and talk about it.
- ◆ Invite your closest friend to lunch this week. Notice how it feels to spend more time with people you enjoy.

Chapter 4

What Do You Love To Do?

Stirring The Inner Sparks

"I would rather fail at what I love than succeed at what I hate."
George Burns

What Do You Love to Do?

One of the best ways to learn about yourself and your dreams is to consider what you love to do. You may be surprised at what you discover about yourself when you take a few minutes to list your favorite activities and how often you do them.

Some people learn that the things they love to do don't cost much money or they're even free! Others realize that it's been a long time since they did these fun things. Often they need to create the time freedom so they can do them more frequently. Some learn how important other people are to them. They actively develop their skills to become better spouses, parents and friends, as well as more effective and caring co-workers and associates.

The happiest and most successful people stay in touch with and pursue their dreams. They spend more of their time being fired up and their enthusiasm shines through all areas of their lives. They have acknowledged their goals and dreams and are doing whatever it takes to accomplish them.

They no longer make excuses why they "can't" do it. Instead, they look for reasons why they *can*. They *delay gratification* on activities that would interfere with progress on their dream. They know that consistently taking action toward their dream will keep them fired up. And they discover, as Jim Rohn has said, *"Dreams put to work create the miracle."* Are you ready, like these people have, to experience some miracles of your own?

Your Favorite Activities

Would you like to learn more about yourself and your dreams? If so, take a piece of paper and list 15 favorite things you enjoy doing for fun. Just allow yourself to randomly jot down ideas. If you come up with more than 15, that's great. Here's an example:

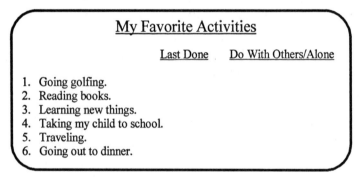

My Favorite Activities

Last Done   Do With Others/Alone

1. Going golfing.
2. Reading books.
3. Learning new things.
4. Taking my child to school.
5. Traveling.
6. Going out to dinner.

Once you have made your list, review it and ask yourself two questions: When did you last do this activity and do you need other people to do it? Write down your answers next to the list. You might consider whether these activities require advance planning, whether they support you mentally or physically, and whether they are structured or unstructured. Like a good detective, take time to really learn about yourself and study your personal preferences. All of this information is quite useful when determining your dreams. Identifying your favorite activities gives significant clues about what you find meaningful and enjoyable.

My Favorite Activities	Last Done	Do With Others/Alone
1. Going golfing.	5 months	with others
2. Reading books.	today	alone
3. Learning new things.	last week	either
4. Taking my child to school.	4 months	alone
5. Traveling.	7 months	with others
6. Going out to dinner.	yesterday	either

Learning About Yourself

As you review your list, you'll probably see a pattern. Say that the things you love to do often require little or no planning. You're probably a spontaneous, fun loving person.

If most of your favorite activities require advance planning, you probably prefer a highly organized lifestyle. You are less likely to do things spontaneously and more likely to plan your life.

If physical risk is involved in most of your favorite activities, you probably prefer excitement over security, freedom over structure and creativity over analysis. If most of your favorite activities are about your physical health, that's a key priority for you and something you value highly. Many of your life choices will be based on whether something is good for you physically. Keeping yourself fit is probably a primary goal in your life.

Study this list and you may learn things about yourself which you might not have known before. Your favorite activities provide valuable clues about what gets you fired up. They say a great deal about your personality and values. Later, we'll discuss how they fit with your life purpose.

One question you need to ask when you look at this list is—*how long it's been since you did the things you love.*

When you do things that get you fired up it's likely that you are often happy and have a cheerful attitude. If you have not done any of your favorite things recently, you may want to treat yourself as a reward for achieving a goal you set.

Picture how great it will be when you can spend more time doing the things you're excited about. Imagine how terrific your life will be when every day you are living your dreams, fired up about your life, doing what you want to do with the people you love and enjoy most!

Blend What You Love to Do With Building Your Business or Profession

A great way to get the most out of your investment in building your business or profession is to mix business with pleasure. Whenever there's a business trip that's out of town, you could go there early or stay longer to see the local attractions. You'll be investing in your future, while enjoying the present. Check your financial situation and schedule before you make your plans.

Now Take These *Are You Fired Up?* Action Steps

♦ Complete the "My Favorite Activities" list.
♦ Read over your list and learn more about yourself.
♦ Schedule in one of your favorite activities as a reward for reaching a goal in your business or profession.
♦ Look at your out-of-town schedule. Consider how you could blend some pleasure in with business by staying a day or two longer.

Chapter 5

Use Your Imagination To Fuel Your Dream

Fueling The Spark Inside

*"The clearer you are about what you want,
the easier it is to make it happen."*

The Fire of Life Is Inside You

You *can* have the life you've always wanted. Since you've gotten this far, it's likely you really do want to make your dreams come true. But maybe you're still not quite sure what your dreams are. In this book, you'll find more ways to help you discover your dreams. Then you can work to make them come true. You'll read about other people like you who did whatever was necessary to live their dreams. Your discovery process can often be easy and fun, and you'll be amazed at how much progress you can make in such a short time. So let yourself enjoy the process; it's all for you!

Are You Fired Up? Principle #5—*Use Your Imagination*

Your imagination is a powerful tool. It can help you resolve tough situations and fuel your dreams. Famous Olympic athletes from all over the world have mentally pictured their success for decades. One study showed that the

East Germans and Russian Olympic athletes spent 75 percent of their training time envisioning their peak performance. That meant they were doing the actual physical training only 25 percent of the time! Today, many professional athletes regularly focus on and imagine their victories; they mentally see themselves winning. Picturing their success helps them to make it a reality.

Dan O'Brien, 1996 Decathlon champion, practiced every day for years to go to the Olympics. In 1992 he faced the heartbreak of not qualifying at the Olympic trials. Dan was determined not to let that happen again! At home, he jogged every day, picturing himself running victoriously through the Olympic stadium.

Dan imagined himself wearing the gold medal and the crowd calling out his name over and over again as he earned the title, "The world's greatest athlete." He called himself that every day, affirming it to himself as *the truth in advance*. With the heart and mind of an Olympian, Dan got fired up for the 1996 Olympics. All of his dreams came true as he won the Decathlon gold medal and reclaimed it for the United States—for the first time in 20 years!

The Clearer You Are, the Easier It Is

The clearer you are about what you want, the easier it is to make it happen. It's essential to clearly define your dreams in vivid detail. However, if your dreams are still fuzzy or even a complete mystery, take heart. You're going to have a chance right now to learn more about your dreams.

One of the best ways to gain more information is to *imagine* each of your dreams fully realized in all its glory. Thomas Edison spent a great deal of dreaming (while awake!) about his life. To stay refreshed and creative, he often took naps and encouraged his employees to do the same. In fact, he got some of his best ideas while daydreaming, focusing on what he wanted to do. That's why it's smart for you to do this as well. It'll help you access the creative part of your brain and gain valuable insight about how your life could be. It will help you get fired up.

Picture What You Want

Take a few minutes now to relax and picture your success. See yourself with all the time and money you'll ever want or need. Picture yourself enjoying more time with your family and friends. Imagine walking the beaches of the world and going places you've always wanted to go, and doing what you've always wanted to do.

Picture yourself living in your dream house, with a maid and a groundskeeper, if that's what you'd like. Imagine having the freedom and ease to come and go as you please, knowing that everything is taken care of.

Now imagine yourself fired up at a big seminar, being recognized on stage because you reached a new level in your business or profession. Sense how terrific you feel, how grateful, how successful. You've been focusing on your goals and you're seeing your dreams coming true!

As you move-on, you may travel and speak at seminars yourself. You'll be able to inspire others and see them enthusiastically respond to your excitement, sincerity and winning track record. Notice how people follow your example and seek your guidance and wisdom. Listen to their comments and questions and give them your best. Watch yourself helping them move-on, making a difference in their lives. You are becoming a great leader.

Now observe how your life has changed. How are you spending your time? Where are you living and who are you surrounding yourself with? Notice how full your life is and how healthy and energized you feel. How does it feel to be financially free and doing what you love to do? What are others saying to you? What are you saying to others? Listen to the happiness and commitment in your voice; feel your passion and sense of purpose. You know your contribution is valuable and meaningful, particularly with your family, friends, and close associates.

What does your life look like? What is happening? How and where are you doing your business or profession, and enjoying your life? Oh yes, they seem like one and the same, don't they? You're having so much fun, it's hard to believe that this is how you've earned your new lifestyle. What does the world look like to you from this perspective? See it clearly. Feel your deep sense of satisfaction and gratitude.

Take your time and experience only good things; see all the positive aspects of your life and feel your own excitement and vitality. Allow your creative imagination to paint a vivid picture; make it real with sounds and smells and colors. Observe the people and feel the emotions. Let your imagination get you fired up. See it all in a positive way as totally fulfilling—and be thankful.

Write Down Your Feelings

After "dreaming" for several minutes, make some notes on your experience. This can be done on paper or by just talking into a tape recorder. Did you know that whatever you "wind" into a tape recorder, you also "wind" into your subconscious? Wouldn't it be powerful to wind success and happiness onto your internal "tapes"? Perhaps you found yourself doing something you never even considered, and you got a new dream along the line. That often happens during this activity.

Note your feelings, actions, family, friends and lifestyle, even if some of it seems unfamiliar to you now. All of this is important information as you gain greater clarity about igniting your internal fire. You may not understand the exact nature of what you were doing; but it just felt right. That's perfectly normal. You probably have more wisdom than you may think. All it takes is the courage to—*start exploring and trusting yourself.*

One couple who did this got such clear ideas about the life they wanted to live (which was very different from their life at the time) that they changed their lives considerably in six months. They envisioned themselves financially free with more time for their family.

After the process, they got moving and started building their own business. As it grew, they found themselves living their lives with more enthusiasm, success and freedom. Soon they were being recognized for their accomplishments, and traveling to prime vacation spots. They didn't realize what their life was really all about until they started following their dream. Prior to that they basically took life for granted. The turning point came when they went forward in faith believing in and imagining their success as clearly as they could picture it.

Now congratulate yourself on your progress so far. Acknowledge yourself for doing these activities and putting positive energy into your life. You're worth it! Enjoy the dream; savor it like your favorite meal. Let it sink in and get richer. It's too new to expose to possible critics, so don't share it with anyone who might try to "burst your bubble." Let it blossom under your tender care. You may even find that you get more ideas as you go along.

Sometimes when you're resting in bed, you may come up with more ideas about your dreams. Be sure to keep a notebook by the bed for just that reason, and write down your ideas. And again, share it only with those closest to you who are also supportive of you. They would be people like your spouse and mentor.

Remind yourself of all the successes you have had in your life until now. You have unique gifts and talents to share with others. Remember—*you were born to win.* Let that get you fired up. Pat yourself on the back for your progress and your new awareness. You're taking action and moving on. Bravo!

Now Take These *Are You Fired Up?* Action Steps

◆ Spend some time dreaming about the success you want. See yourself living your dream.

◆ Write down your dream in detail and refer to it often. You may also want to record your dream on tape and listen to it often.

◆ Create a success notebook of all the major accomplishments you've had in your life until now. Include childhood learning like how to ride a bike or confronting the neighborhood bully. Give yourself credit for all that you have accomplished so far, but don't rest on your laurels. Keep going!

Chapter 6

What Are Your Myths?

Dousing The Sparks

"If people don't have a positive influence in their lives to show them that challenges are just a part of learning and growing, they often develop myths that limit their belief in themselves and steal their dreams."

False Beliefs Are Dreamstealers

Why do some people achieve their dreams, while many don't? One of the greatest dreamstealers is *doubt*. In many cases, people allow the limiting beliefs they learned during childhood, or even later in life, to stop them from taking that extra step. False beliefs often keep them from stretching outside their comfort zone and taking risks to make their dreams come true. They buy into false beliefs i.e., myths, which could lead them to sabotage their own success.

Are You Fired Up? **Principle #6—***Uncover Your Myths*

People often learn myths through childhood or some unpleasant life experiences which restrict their thinking and hold them back. Sometimes parents unintentionally pass along incorrect information like: "If you don't get a good education, you'll never amount to anything," or "Keep your nose to the grindstone and you shoulder to the wheel," or "If you want to get ahead in this world, you have to know the right people."

Your parents weren't intentionally trying to set up blocks for you. They probably believed they were motivating you with what they thought was true. And it's likely you believed all of this to be true without question. And since your subconscious can't evaluate, it just accepted it.

If people don't have a positive influence in their lives to show them that the *challenges are just part of learning and growing,* they often develop myths that limit their belief in themselves and steal their dreams. Instead of viewing each obstacle as a necessary step in the overall process of success, if people stumble, they may label themselves failures, and believe they can't win. They may have no one to encourage them over the hurdles.

During adolescence, they may have been taught other destructive myths like: "I'm not good enough," "I can't have what I want," or "Nobody likes me or my ideas." While these myths may seem to provide some protection or consolation during youth, they're rarely constructive in adulthood. Sometimes myths become deeply ingrained in the subconscious, where they are most dangerous. They can cause people to destroy their possibilities for success by giving up on their dreams and making excuses. And, most people don't realize this is happening because it's become a self-defeating habit.

Discover what myths you're telling yourself and replace these with positive affirmations to help you succeed. You'll be happier and healthier, as well. (We'll discuss affirmations later.) *Your awareness of your myths is your key to letting them go.* You are likely to be amazed to learn what untruths may be dwelling in your subconscious. Take the time to investigate. Learn to laugh at your myths and release their negative hold on you.

Here are three action options to help you learn more about your own false beliefs. Each one is short and fun, and can help you be more successful. Choose the activity that appeals to you most.

Step 1/Action Option A—*Talk With Your Leader or Mentor*

Talk with your leader or mentor who's understanding and supportive as well as a good listener. Family members can often know you too well, or so they may think. Sit down with your mentor and just talk about your dream and what is stopping you from living it right now, today, in this very moment. Record the myths that show up while you talk. Make a list of them. Continue sharing until you believe you have covered all the possible blocks to your success. Now go to Step 2 on page 45.

Step 1/Action Option B—*Review Your Personal History*

Find a nice, quiet place where you won't be disturbed, and turn on some soft soothing music. It's likely you have already been a success in many areas of your life. But right now, you need to look at your disappointments. Think back over your life and look at the goals and dreams you have not achieved.

Pay attention to the limiting beliefs (myths) that may have held you back. Decide if you're still allowing them to have "power" over you.

One way to do this is to say the myth out loud and notice whether you feel upset in your stomach or just uneasy. If so, you're still letting these beliefs have power over you. If you just laugh or have no reaction, then your belief no longer affects you. Make a written list of those you still find difficult to think about. Now go to Step 2 on page 45.

Step 1/Action Option C—*The Dreamstealer Checklist*
Listed below are several common dreamstealing thoughts. People often let them get in the way of living their dreams, by using them as excuses. Read over the list and check off those you believe are true for you. Write down those that you have *allowed* to have power over you and add any new ones. Now go to Step 2 on page 45.

Checklist: Checkmark any that ring true for you.

_____ People who live their dreams have to be rich.

_____ People who live their dreams must be well-educated and have college degrees.

_____ People who live their dreams have to be well-connected.

_____ People who live their dreams are selfish.

_____ People who live their dreams have to be healthy and fit.

_____ People who live their dreams have a lot of free time.

_____ People who live their dreams have to be 100 percent confident at all times.

_____ People who live their dreams have to be well-organized.

_____ People who live their dreams must have loads of energy.

_____ People who live their dreams are always unusually talented.

_____ People who live their dreams are always very intelligent.

_____ People who live their dreams must be fearless.

_____ People who live their dreams must take risks.

_____ People who live their dreams are always good-looking.

_____ People who live their dreams must be young (or old).

_____ People who live their dreams must have independent sources of income.

_____ People who live their dreams don't have time for their families.

_____ People who live their dreams have to be totally unique.
_____ People who live their dreams have their "act together" (always know exactly what they are doing).
_____ People who live their dreams have to be a certain sex or race.
_____ People who live their dreams are (fill in the blanks)_____

_____

Once you have completed one of the action options, are you ready to laugh about your dreamstealing beliefs? Do you realize how untrue they really are and that they have no power over you?

Step 2—*Laugh a Little*

Someone once said, "Laughter is the best medicine." It can help you get a new perspective on the myths you have allowed to get in the way of you living your dreams up until now. Look over your list and notice how silly some of these beliefs are. Some of them even contradict each other. Some make no sense at all.

Without exception, I can give you examples of real-life people who prove every one of these myths is false. So relax and laugh a little at the words. Soon they'll have no power over you because you will have let them go, eliminating their hold on you.

Step 3—*Let the Myths Go*

Whichever action option you picked, you need to have a piece of paper with the myths written on it that you have allowed to affect you. Here are two of the many ways you can let them go:

#1—For each myth you have written, write a positive statement in its place that invalidates it. See the following example:

MYTH—People need to be well-educated and have college degrees to live their dreams.

POSITIVE TRUE STATEMENT—People of any educational level can live their dreams.

After you have done this for *each* myth, go to #2.

#2—Draw a big "X" through the list of myths.

If it gives you more satisfaction, individually cross each myth out. Next, tear up that piece of paper into tiny pieces while saying out loud, *"I permanently let go of these limiting beliefs. I am now free to make my dreams come true."* If you like, you can also burn those pieces of paper, symbolically destroying the myths. While this may sound a bit silly, *it works!* It can be quite powerful. Feel the relief that comes when you are no longer carrying that emotional garbage. Let it all go, and get on with your life.

Are You Fired Up? Principle #7—*Identify Role Models*

To succeed in life, we all need excellent role models—people who beat the odds and won. They show us that if they can make it, so can we. These people need not be big, famous heroes; it could be the child with a mental or physical challenge who finally got on the baseball team. Or it could be a local physically challenged person who's inspiring other people to overcome their obstacles. Or it may be the bus driver, who has won safety and courtesy awards, who called you by your name every morning and said you could do anything you decided to do.

Take a minute now to think about the inspirational role models in your life. Who are they? Are they well-known people in or out of your field of endeavor, or are they relatively unknown people like a close friend, your teacher, your mother or father, your grandmother or grandfather, or your next door neighbor? What did they do for you? How did they touch your life? Oftentimes, you'll discover that it was all the little things they did for you throughout the years that made the difference, not necessarily something big.

When you are working on your dream, it helps to contact those people who inspire you. Tell them how they touched your life and thank them. Everyone, no matter how famous, loves to hear sincere feedback about how they made a difference in the lives of others. When you share with them from your heart, chances are they'll encourage you even more.

From my early years on, my grandmother McClamroch was a tremendous role model for me. Her parents were killed in a car crash when she was 12, and she went to live with an aunt and uncle. Going through such tough times emotionally and financially taught her to be self-reliant. She went to Goucher College and later married a college professor from another university.

While her husband was in the U.S. Army during World Wars I and II, she organized the local women, made bandages and kept things going at home. She beat several different kinds of cancer before she died in her mid-70's. Her courage and perseverance strongly influenced me. By her example, she showed me how to overcome my challenging childhood and keep moving towards my dreams.

Talk With a Leader Who's a Hero to You

"___(Name)___, I just want you to know that I admire you for the way you have built your success and care about people. It's obvious you're a great leader, and I know that I could learn a lot from you. I'm serious about my future and will do whatever it takes to make it happen. Would you have time to counsel me? I'd really appreciate it."

Another way you could start would be "___(Name)___, your recent seminar really touched my heart. It's amazing how you overcame so many obstacles to get where you are. You have really inspired me to learn how to better support and encourage others. Would you be in a position to counsel me and give me some guidance? I will follow your advice. I really think you could help me and I would very much appreciate your time."

Approaches like these are powerful and effective. Everyone who has succeeded has overcome many challenges. They can relate to your needs when you show them respect, courtesy and sincere admiration. Always honor their time and stick to the main issues. Leaders always welcome those who are serious about making their dreams come true. You'll be delighted with how helpful they can be.

Leaders feel honored and humbled when someone calls or writes to tell them how they have touched their lives. If you're already a leader, you'll understand.

Are You Fired Up? Principle #8—*Listen to Motivational Tapes and Attend Seminars*

Another way to stay fired up while you're working on your dream is *listening to motivational audiotapes every day.* Perhaps your company or organization has or can recommend a continuing education tape program you could take advantage of. It's been said that to fully benefit from a tape, you need to listen to it seventeen times. Play it at home while you get ready for work, and before you go to bed. Make your car a "university on wheels." Simply insert the tapes into your tape player and press "play" for your success!

Going to motivational seminars can also help you overcome your obstacles and succeed. They can help you to stay on track and accelerate your success. I've been going to seminars for years, and they really help. Doing so helped keep me motivated as I built my business.

Just one word or sentence heard on a tape or at a seminar could ignite a spark inside you and get you fired up. The entire price of the seminar, or listening to a hundred tapes, would be more than worth it! Keep doing what it takes to stay motivated. You never know when your sparks will ignite a fire.

Another benefit of seminars and tapes is having what we already believe to be confirmed by others. Then you don't feel so alone and you know you're on track. For example, the speaker may share how they overcame a certain obstacle that you may be experiencing right now. Associating with other like-minded people who are also moving on traveling a similar path, can inspire and motivate you. And of course, the tremendous energy of being in a room with others who are fired up can light your fire, too!

Are You Fired Up? **Principle #9—***Act "As If"*

One of the best ways to get fired up about your dream and ignite your sparks is to act as if your dream is already your reality. First, your dream needs to come alive in your mind and heart before it can come true. So an essential part of the process is acting as if your dream is already a part of your life.

For example, when I was building my house, I visited it every week, imagining what it would feel like to live there. Driving your dream car or visiting your dream house can make your flames burn higher and brighter. Even *dressing the part* of the dream you want to live can change the way you feel about yourself.

Start acting as if your dream is real. The more vividly you can see, hear and experience your dream, the more likely you are to realize it. This helps you to become more familiar with your dream, creating a new belief level that you can do it. You've already integrated this new experience into your life and your mind. Your dream then becomes your new comfort zone. As a result, it seems like the natural thing to do is to go to your next level of success, which is making it really happen.

The late Florence Griffith Joyner, super sprinter of the 1988 Olympics, used clothes as a key tool for acting "as if." Wearing brightly colored running outfits and beautifully painted fingernails, Florence won three gold medals. *"My outfits represent the belief, determination, discipline and desire to make my dreams come true...."*

Congratulations on your progress. You've made a great start by letting go of your myths. *You deserve to have whatever your heart desires.* Keep moving!

Now Take These *Are You Fired Up?* Action Steps

♦ Do the myths activity.
♦ Write a letter or talk to your leader or mentor who is a hero to you, describing how they inspire you. Ask if you may talk with them about making your dream come true.
♦ Get on a continuing education program of listening to motivational tapes. Listen to at least one tape a day.
♦ Attend motivational and leadership seminars regularly.

Chapter 7

Dream, Vision, Mission, and Purpose

Laying The Core Logs

*"Rise above previous 'limitations' and do more than
you ever thought possible."*

Where Does Your Dream Begin?

As you begin focusing more on what *you* want, you may
wonder "How do I begin to define my dreams?" An excellent
place to start is with your life vision, mission and purpose.

Your vision, mission, and purpose all relate to your values
and what you consider important. In Dr. Martin Luther King
Jr.'s famous 1960's speech titled *I Have A Dream*, his
purpose and mission were very clear. He envisioned a world
where the United States would *"...one day rise up and live
out its creed...that all men are created equal...where my
children will not be judged by the color of their skin, but
rather by the content of their character,"* and *"...where black
men and white men, Jews and Gentiles, Protestants and
Catholics will be able to join hands and say 'free at last, free
at last. Thank God Almighty, we are free at last.'"*

That got him fired up and led him to inspire millions of
people, even decades later. Whenever I watch a video of him
delivering that speech, I can feel his passion. He was an
exceptional man who lived and died for his principles.

Your life purpose can be a great driving force, too. It can help you break through any barriers that may have been in your mind and in your environment. It can move you to rise above previous "limitations" and do more than you ever thought possible.

Vision, Mission and Purpose

Your *vision* is the loftiest expression of what you truly want for your life. It is your mental picture of hope and optimism, of the ideal. You may be familiar with Ralph Waldo Emerson's famous words, "Where there is no vision, the people perish."

Your life purpose relates to what you are meant to do in your life, as you feel it in your heart.

A *mission statement* reflects what and how you contribute to the world. It is based on how you are implementing your life purpose.

A vision would relate more to how the owner would like their business to be in the future. You might have a vision for your business or profession to spread around the world, impacting people everywhere in a positive way.

Purpose is the core of both the mission and the vision. It is often found in the heart and soul of the business founder. Perhaps he or she lost a parent to an illness that could have been treated with the right products, so the founder wants to offer products which can help save other people's lives. Or maybe the founder has a burning desire to excel and make a difference; this will have a large impact on how the business is conducted. Doing your purpose will make you feel good about yourself, because you'll be serving others the best way that you can, in line with your talents and abilities.

It's All About Values

Fundamental to vision, mission and purpose are your core values. Values are the qualities you consider most significant and they have tremendous impact on your dreams. They shape your attitudes, beliefs and relationships. Know what you value most when planning your ideal life. Start by including what is most important to you. So what are your core values?

Here's a list of values that may apply to you:

1. *Financial Security*—having the money to handle your economic responsibilities; using it wisely and keeping yourself free from money related difficulties.
2. *Safety*—having physical, emotional or mental protection where you feel free from attack and danger.
3. *Freedom*—having the opportunity and independence to live the life you choose.
4. *Success*—progressively realizing a worthwhile dream or goal.
5. *Joy*—feeling effective, successful, happy and fulfilled.
6. *Love*—having healthy caring relationships with family, friends and associates, especially with that special life long one who you have a committed marital relationship with.
7. *Good Health*—staying physically, emotionally, and mentally sound.
8. *Personal Integrity*—conducting your life honestly, doing what you believe in.
9. *Service*—helping and contributing to the lives of others.
10. *Peace of Mind*—feeling a sense of serenity and freedom from negative stress.
11. *Ease*—a sense of relaxation and comfort.
12. *Spirituality*—matters relating to belief in God. Your faith.
13. *Creativity*—freely expressing your talents and abilities however you choose.

14. *Personal growth*—continually refining and developing your inner qualities, learning from your mistakes and moving on.
15. *Greatness*—making a significant impact on the world, sometimes leading to public recognition and awareness of who you are on a large scale.
16. *Humility*—being aware of your unskilled behavior, based on your understanding that no one succeeds alone. Having no unhealthy pride.
17. *Order*—dealing with your environment so everything is structured and well-organized.
18. *Humor*—being able to laugh with others and not take yourself too seriously.
19. *Talent*—natural ability to learn or do a specific skill or art form.

Values Activity

Add any other values to the ones just listed which are important to you. List in order of priority from 1 to 5 which of the values are most important to you. Most important would be #1.

1._____ 2._____

3._____ 4._____

5._____

Now study your list. It will provide a great deal of useful data for you. Your top five values will shape your life decisions the most and give you the best clues about what really gets you fired up.

Discovering Your Life Purpose

Believe it or not, discovering your life purpose can be easy. And it can actually be broken down into a simple, clear statement.

Be aware that you may have more than one purpose, which you could express in a variety of ways. For example, you could express your purpose in several different ways. Here are three possibilities, one of which may fit you: caring about others and sharing your success ideas with them to help them live their dreams; to use profits from your business or profession to establish a foundation and home for underprivileged children; or to build a chain of restaurants to serve people healthy foods.

The key is to be open and flexible. Imagine you are a private detective and the subject of your investigation is your life. You gather as many clues as possible, put them all down on paper and make sense out of them. You'll discover the answers when you persist and take it one step at a time. You may find this a fascinating and profound experience. For many people, it comes as a tremendous relief to know why they are here on this Earth and to discover what is truly meaningful to them.

Your Life Purpose Worksheet

The following worksheet takes you through a series of questions to help you develop your life purpose statement. Take about 15 minutes with this form. If it's not convenient now, do it a little later. This is a very special process. Do it when you can focus on it and allow the information to sink in.

You discover your life purpose by knowing what you love to do, what gets you fired up and what makes you unique. What you love to do is clearly an expression of your values. It's as simple as that.

Step 1—*What Are Your Best and Most Unique Qualities?*

List your best and most unique qualities, and then pick the two that reflect who you are and for which you would most like to be remembered. In the first example on the previous page, your best and most unique qualities are leadership and caring about people.

Your Life Purpose Worksheet

Step 1: List your best and most unique qualities. Which two qualities truly reflect who you are and for which you'd most like to be remembered? Underline these two.

Step 2: List several ways you enjoy expressing or sharing those two qualities. Use action verbs with "ing" endings. Underline your two favorite forms of expression.

Step 3: Describe your version of an ideal world.

Step 4: Combine the three steps above into one sentence that summarizes your life purpose.

Ex. I am <u>encouraging</u> and <u>leading</u> others with my <u>positive example</u> so that everyone <u>contributes for the greatest benefit of all.</u>

As you identify your particular qualities, start first with a list of what you believe are all of your best traits. Then go back and underline the two that you feel most uniquely represent you. If you still aren't sure, ask a supportive family member or friend what they think your best and most unique traits are.

These are often the qualities that people frequently comment on. They are the traits without which you would not be uniquely you.

Step 2—*How Do You Enjoy Expressing Those Traits?*

List all your favorite ways of expressing those qualities, using verbs ending in "ing." Then pick your top two favorite forms of expression.

For the first example on the previous page, your two favorites were helping people by sharing your success ideas with them.

After you list several forms of expression you enjoy, choose your top two. Go back and review them one by one, and see which words really feel right to you, and which ways you most enjoy expressing those traits. You may want to ask for help from a supportive loved one if you need it. They may recognize something about you that you may not.

When you express yourself in these two favorite ways, you feel happy and have a sense of positive well-being, delight and freedom.

Note that if there is any resistance at all to a word, then that is probably not your favorite form of expressing or sharing your two best and most unique qualities. Here's how your Life Purpose Worksheet could look:

Your Life Purpose Worksheet

Step 1: List your best and most unique qualities. Which two qualities truly reflect who you are and for which you'd most like to be remembered? Underline these two.

leadership, caring, humor, flexibility, teaching ability

Step 2: List several ways you enjoy expressing or sharing those two qualities. Use action verbs with "ing" endings. Underline your two favorite forms of expression.

Sharing success ideas, helping people, teaching, flying, skiing, running.

Step 3: Describe your version of an ideal world.

It's a peaceful, healthy world where people use free enterprise to help each other live their dreams.

Step 4: Combine the three steps above into one sentence that summarizes your life purpose.

Ex. I am sharing success ideas and helping others succeed. I am demonstrating my caring for others as I express my leadership and inspire others to grow personally and become financially free in a world where people are living their dreams.

Step 3—*What's Your Ideal World?*

Here you simply describe what your ideal world would be like if you could design it. This is a vision statement, because it has hope, optimism and a statement of the ideal in it. Include what you believe are the most vital elements. What would address world problems that most disturb you? What would ensure a positive world for the future? These are all *your* choices and *your* opinions. That's all that matters here.

So it's best not to consult anyone else on this question, or you may be influenced by their idea of a perfect world.

Now you're almost done. You know what makes you unique and your favorite ways of expressing that uniqueness. You also have defined your ideal world. All of this information forms the foundation of your life purpose.

Now look over what could be your Life Purpose Worksheet on the previous page and read the answers to each of the questions. For you, an ideal world is healthy, peaceful and one where everyone helps each other and uses free enterprise to live their dreams.

Your leadership and caring are your most unique traits, and your favorite forms of expressing those traits are by sharing your success ideas and helping people. Putting all those together into Step 4, one sentence which combines all the above information, "you" came up with your life purpose:

"I am sharing success ideas and helping others succeed. I am demonstrating my caring for others as I express my leadership and inspire others to grow personally and become financially free in a world where people are living their dreams." See how easily this all fits together? *Yours* can, too.

Step 4—*Summarize Your Life Purpose Statement*

Combine all the elements of the last three questions into one single life purpose statement. There are several ways to start. One is to begin with "I am" and then drop in the two verbs. Example: "I am sharing success ideas and helping others succeed."

Another way is to write "Using my" then add your two qualities and follow with "I am...so that others may..." Example: "Using my leadership and caring, I am sharing success ideas and helping others succeed in a way that inspires others to grow personally and become financially free."

Yet a third way might be to show how your life's purpose assists the world as a whole. In the example we're using here, you believe sharing your success ideas will "inspire others to grow personally and become financially free." Whichever way works best for you is the right way. How about completing your Life Purpose Worksheet now?

Here are some other examples of life purpose statements: These are all from ordinary people. They are not blessed with any special gifts that make them more likely to succeed than others. They are simply fired up about their dreams:

Ed, a national trainer who works with youth, developed this life purpose statement: "As a loving, courageous and compassionate man, I inspire the youth of today through fun and enthusiasm and have tremendous impact on their lives." His vision is a world of children who feel good about themselves and are confident and productive members of society. His mission is to teach youth leadership skills with excellence and enthusiasm.

Will, an American working in Bulgaria, writes his life purpose statement: "Honestly and clearly sharing my life experiences and knowledge, I am creating and promoting world community and peace." His vision is a world which is one large community, respecting and appreciating each other's uniqueness. His mission is to bring business tools and techniques to budding entrepreneurs in undeveloped parts of the world and assist them in becoming financially independent.

As you read over these statements, it's obvious how distinct each one is. Each person finds a unique way to express their purpose and have a meaningful, fulfilling life—just like you're doing. As you achieve various goals and realize certain dreams, your expression may change.

However, you can use your life purpose statement as a key reference point throughout your life, especially when you are making major decisions and planning each year. Your true happiness depends on living your life's activities in tune with your life purpose.

You might want to share your life purpose statement with someone you love and trust, like your leader or mentor. You could copy it onto a 3" x 5" index card and carry it in your wallet, day planner or date book. You could also tape it to your bathroom mirror to remind you why you're here. Whatever you choose to do, *honor it and yourself.* There's only one you! You are a rare individual with treasured gifts that only you can express in exactly your way.

Now Take These *Are You Fired Up?* Action Steps

♦ Identify your values using the list in this chapter.
♦ Complete the life purpose questions in this chapter.
♦ Copy your life purpose on an index card. Always carry it with you and also put it where you will see it often. Honor it and yourself.
♦ This week, be sure to schedule time attending to the things you truly value. For example, if financial freedom is really important to you, invest your time building your business or profession so you can achieve it. If excellent health is a priority for you, then schedule time to exercise in a way that you enjoy. Perhaps you can take regular brisk walks and blend it with your financial freedom priority. Listen to a continuing education tape on your portable tape player as you walk.
♦ If you are inspired by Dr. Martin Luther King, Jr. you may want to watch a video of his *I Have A Dream* speech.

Chapter 8

Putting It All Together

Expanding The Fire's Foundation

"Events and circumstances...have their origin in ourselves.
They spring from seeds which we have sown."
Henry David Thoreau

Do What You Love and Love What You Do

You'll find your life purpose and favorite activities relate to each other. It makes sense. What you love doing gives you the most satisfaction and gets you the most fired up. They are usually right on target with your life purpose.

Relating what you love doing with your life purpose can give you some terrific ideas of how to have a more fulfilling and happy life. What you most enjoy reflects your values, and demonstrates how these values affect your behavior. Notice that things you avoid, or would like to avoid, are probably in conflict with your life purpose.

That's why so many people are unhappy at work. In many cases, their work doesn't support their life purpose and values; therefore, it doesn't fulfill them. If this is true for you, once you realize this, you'll become more hopeful that your life could be more meaningful. You'll have discovered a key piece of your life "puzzle" and, perhaps, the main missing piece preventing you from ultimate happiness and success.

Like millions of others around the world, you have chosen to build your business or profession so you can achieve your dreams and goals and life purpose. If what you're now doing conflicts with your life purpose, you need to take action to realize your ultimate potential.

One Woman's Journey Toward Living Her Dream

One young woman found that her job was in conflict with her life purpose. Armed with new awareness and a heartfelt desire to succeed, she started building her own business. She no longer dreads work, and is actually a better employee. She knows that her job is only a "stepping stone" on her journey of success. Her attitude has shifted dramatically, so much so that her co-workers have commented on how upbeat and happy she now seems.

By knowing her life purpose, values and preferred activities, she is consistently taking the action necessary to replace her income, enabling her to live in integrity with herself and her values. When she does, she'll be able to live her dream.

Getting "The Big Picture"

Awareness is powerful. For many people, just the act of relating their favorite activities with their life purpose gives them much greater clarity about their life vision. Suddenly, their dream becomes crystal clear. They are enthusiastic, ready to move on and make their vision a reality. Perhaps that's where you are right now; if so, congratulations!

You now have dreams you can work toward; dreams that can inspire you to master the tools for success and a "vehicle" you can use to make them come true. It's likely you're in the best position ever to really make it happen for you and your family.

Are You Fired Up? **Principle #10—*Take Action and Keep Moving***

No dream was ever accomplished without taking action. You need to move and do, following a proven pattern for success, to make things happen. If you're still unsure about your dream, remember to *take action anyway.* When you move, one way or another, you'll get feedback.

You might want to adopt the idea of *ready-fire-aim.* When things go well, you are on track and what you're doing reflects your purpose. If things don't work and you're unhappy and out of balance, it's likely that you are not living according to your purpose. You need to aim again. This feedback is valuable. Learn from it. Determine what you need to do next, ask for help when necessary, and go forward. Keep building your business or profession and moving towards your dream of doing what you love to do— one step at a time and one day at a time.

Those who don't take action simply stagnate. They sit at home, out of work, on unemployment compensation or welfare, or in an ungratifying dead-end career, and they "die" inside. They complain and refuse to take responsibility for actions that got them where they are. Instead, they blame others. They may even throw a "pity party."

But guess what? Nobody comes! You may know some people like this. Insulate yourself from their negativity. By their refusal to move on, they become their own worst enemy. Doing something worthwhile requires thought and purpose, and often means the person needs to stop feeling sorry for themselves. Until they begin taking positive action, they won't start to truly live or happily fulfill their purpose.

Andrew Shue, the actor, created a nonprofit organization for young people called "Do Something." Young people apply for grants from this organization to do local community projects. Shue's organization has positively influenced many youngsters around the U.S., and serves as a great role model for others. He believes "the bottom line" is that people need to take action, to "*Do Something,*" so things can get better.

Maybe you have written out your life purpose. You may have developed a short statement describing your dream—explaining exactly how you want to live. If so, that's terrific! You're probably fired up about it. Focus on your dream statement for a while and see, feel and hear it happening. After reflection, you may want to change it a bit, and that's fine.

As you're striving for it, your dream is always "a work in progress." It grows as you grow and become. Only share this dream with your leader or mentor or supportive spouse. This is a deeply personal and private statement and one that may be new and tender to you—like an infant. Protect it and keep it close to your heart. Don't tell negative-thinking people about your dream. They could be jealous of you and try to douse the flames of your fire.

The immense value of knowing your life purpose is shown in this story. A highly-respected doctor who has been enormously successful found that he was getting burned-out. He had money, success and fame. What he really wanted and loved to do, though, was spend more time with his family. He was working almost all the time to give his wife and children a lifestyle he'd personally never have.

So one day, he started building another business and, in two years, replaced his income. He was able to leave his medical practice and now has the time and energy to do what he wants with the people he loves. As he discovered, life is much more meaningful when you live it in line with your purpose.

We all live in accordance with our philosophy of life, which determines how our life develops. Just as in sailing, when the way the sail is set determines which way the boat goes, a person's mindset determines the direction of their life.

If you don't know what your vision is by now, that's okay. *Keep moving anyway.* Pick a practice dream to use for taking action. It could be something you really want, even though it may not be your ultimate dream. It might be just one small part of it, or it might be a goal you've had for some time and haven't yet completed. It needs to have meaning and value for you; one that excites you enough to achieve it.

Using this practice dream will give you the opportunity to learn about taking action with tools that can be applied to any dream or goal in your life. The important thing is you need to focus on something positive—*something to aim for.*

If you're not sure what your ultimate dream is, take a moment now to verbalize and write down a practice dream. Start with the two words "I am" and then use "ing" verbs to complete the sentence. (It may help you to review the Life Purpose guidelines in Chapter 7.) Rewrite the sentence until it feels right. Keep it fairly short so you can easily remember it. Once you have it, keep it where you'll see it often.

Whether you are working with your ultimate life dream or your practice dream, you now have a statement which you can refer to and turn into reality. Great! You persisted, created a result, and you now have a track to run on. That's what realizing your dream is all about—doggedly persevering, focusing and taking action on it, until you make it a reality. Remember, as Helen Keller once said, *"One can never consent to creep when one feels an impulse to soar."*

Now Take These *Are You Fired Up?* Action Steps

♦ Relate your favorite activities in your life purpose statement. Make sure they fit.

♦ Write a "dream statement" of something you truly want which is in tune with your life purpose and favorite activities. You can use a smaller dream to practice with.

♦ Spend some time mentally picturing your dream in as much detail as possible, as if it is totally real and you are now living it.

Chapter 9

The Dream Creates Action

Laying The Best Kindling

"(Take) action. Seize the moment..."
Theodore Roosevelt

Are You Fired Up? **Principle #11—***Have a Plan*

The most successful ventures occur because of planning and action. DisneyWorld succeeded because after Walt flew over the swamps of Florida, he envisioned the entire concept and went back and made a plan. He got a team together and took action. In his imagination, he knew what DisneyWorld would look like one, three, five, ten and even twenty years later. He had a magnificent plan for the future and it worked

In this chapter, you will build on your dream and develop a plan for achieving it. Ideas not acted on become unfinished business and cause frustrations. Ideas put into practice can result in incredible outcomes, victories and inventions. The telephone, television and computer were all the result of ideas put into action. So were the airplane and automobile.

None of those inventions would exist if their inventors hadn't had a plan where they continually took action, learned from their mistakes and made adjustments. Now's the time for you to take action toward achieving your dream. As Thomas Edison said, *"The value of an idea lies in the using of it."*

Your Dream Is Your Catalyst for Success

Always remember that while dreams are absolutely essential for you to move ahead and give your life meaning, it's *what you become in the process* that's most important. If you become a wealthy person by using people, you'll be very lonely and disliked. However, when you consistently help enough others realize their dream, you'll automatically achieve yours. And many people will love and respect you all the way to the top.

Here's a brief description of how having a dream leads to success: The dream creates action. By taking action we overcome fear. In overcoming fear, we develop faith and strength. With faith and strength, we build belief in ourselves. As our belief increases, we gain confidence. With confidence, we develop self-esteem and think bigger. Applying all these, we get *results* which lead to our success.

Using the *Are You Fired Up?* Action Plan for Dreambuilding

This is a valuable tool that you can use over and over again to build a dream and develop a plan for making it come true. It'll help you get moving on your dreams in a concrete, practical way. All too often, people have great dreams but never make a plan for achieving them. Cemeteries are full of them. And the world is deprived of untold great ideas. You don't want that to happen to you. Start *moving* today. A good place to begin is by completing this part of your *action* plan.

Are You Fired Up? Action Plan for Dreambuilding

Name_____Date_____

My Dream (Positively Stated as a Choice, Specific, Powerful, Emotionally Fulfilling)_____
_____
_____

Where I envision this dream 1 year, 3 years, 5 years from now
1 year:_____
3 years:_____
5 years:_____

Get your notes out from Chapter 7 where you did the life purpose worksheet. First fill in the top section called "My Dream." This is where you write a brief, vivid description of your dream. State it positively in the present tense, specifically detailing what you are doing and how you are seeing, hearing and feeling it. Use descriptive words so you get *fired up!* Write it down as clearly as possible. Be sure it's something you really want. Remember, the test for whether you really want something is this. Just ask yourself the question: "If I could have it right now, would I really take it?" If the answer is yes, you do want it. If the answer is no or not now, don't put your energy into it.

Look over your notes from the process you just did and let your mind go back to what you pictured you were doing and what was happening. Be sure to write it as though it were happening right now. Things we write in future tense almost never happen because they stay in the future! We only have today; tomorrow is always in the future. Picture it as if it is happening right *now*—in the present.

Describe the development of your dream one, three and five years from now. Pay attention to whatever ideas pop into your head and jot them down in the space provided on the action plan. If you aren't sure how the dream will unfold, just make it up and have fun with it.

What kinds of things would you like to have happening five years from now? Who would you like to be working with? What do you want the quality of your life to be like? Look ahead to three years from now. What do you want to happen by that time? How is your dream developing towards that five-year picture? Then look at one year from now. What actions have you taken? How is the dream growing and taking shape? Remember, you are just playing with ideas at this point; you are not making any commitments. So let yourself DREAM BIG and create a wonderfully fulfilling vision of the life you want.

One person completed the top of the *Are You Fired Up?* Action Plan for Dreambuilding. In his vision, his new business utilized his leadership and imagination to work with an excited and cooperative team of associates. As he mapped out his one, three and five-year plans, he envisioned his business growing steadily from 100 to 1500 to 10,000 people. He saw himself developing several associates into strong leaders, serving their clients and gaining financial freedom. Since he completed the form, he has enthusiastically started building his business, following through on his strategic plan.

As you do this, be clear and specific about how you want your dream to feel, look and sound one, three and five years from now. Use your imagination. Your life can be even better than your biggest dreams; it just takes enthusiasm, planning and consistent action until you make each dream come true.

Your life may already be exactly how you want it in many areas, but you might want to make some minor adjustments so you can do more of what you enjoy doing the most. If that's the case, great—just picture your life exactly as you want it to be in all areas and notice where you need to make some changes. You may not need to make a big change—it can be as simple as developing enough additional income to reach an education fund goal for sending your children to college. Or you may want to increase the monthly income you'll receive when you retire from your job so you can travel more.

If you do want to make significant changes and start living your life with more fulfillment, realizing you greatest dreams, *you can do that, too.* The *Are You Fired Up?* Action Plan for Dreambuilding can help you make your dreams come true, whatever they may be, because it helps you focus your energy in the right direction.

Now Take These *Are You Fired Up?* Action Steps

♦ If you have not done so already, complete the top part of the *Are You Fired Up?* Action Plan for Dreambuilding in this chapter.

♦ Copy your dream description with one, three and five year goal statements and put it where you will see it every day.

♦ Keep a record of those dreams you want now, and those you may not want until several years from now. As time passes, some things may lose their importance to you, and you'll remove them from your dream list altogether.

Chapter 10

Build Your Business Or Profession To Make Your Dreams Come True

Building The Fire

"Make big plans for big dreams—plans that excite you and stir you into action. Then map out what you need to do to build your business or profession to make those dreams come true."

Ideas Come to You in a Creative Way

Have you ever watched a group of small children spontaneously playacting a scene? They gather leaves, for example, transform them into a fort and create fictional characters for each child to act out. Each has input, and they frequently blurt out their ideas as they pop into their heads. What generally results is a highly imaginative, satisfying game that is absorbing and fun. Adults are like that too.

We don't think in a linear, organized fashion. While outlining is good for presenting ideas in an orderly, formal manner, it's not that useful until we've done the real thinking. Ideas pop in and out of our minds, some of which can take us in entirely new directions. This is where some of your best creative thinking can occur. As you act on your dreams, capturing these creative thoughts is key. Keep a pen and paper or tape recorder with you at all times so you can save your ideas—you never know when they'll show up.

Are You Fired Up? Principle #12—*Capture Your Creativity on Paper*

A mind map is a great way to view the actions you need to take to build your business or profession. It's literally a map of the things you need to do to make your dreams come true. It looks like a chart with several branches going in different directions with your main objective in the center.

This concept is widely used by many training organizations. It originated in the United Kingdom with Tony Buzan. He was inspired by Leonardo DaVinci, one of the greatest thinkers in history, and his approach to taking notes! He called it a mind map.

A mind map allows you to capture both your planned and seemingly random "popcorn" ideas quickly and easily. It provides a great springboard for even more spontaneous imagination. Using it often can help you be a more balanced thinker, utilizing both the emotional and logical sides of your brain, as Leonardo did. Since your mind pictures things, a mind map will help you determine the steps you need to take to accomplish your goals and make your dreams come true.

Many large corporations use this tool for planning and flowchart development. In fact, there is a training company in the Midwestern U.S. that specializes in what they call graphic mind maps. They include pictures and symbols rather than words, since this approach can catch many different ideas.

By using colored markers and construction paper, you can make your mind map even more comprehensive. Some businesses use brown craft paper, taped over walls when they're searching for solutions. That way several people can participate and spin off each other's ideas.

Walt Disney used this concept brilliantly with storyboards and continuous input from his employees. This technique works so well that *The Hunchback of Notre Dame*, one of Disney's animated films, was created in exactly the same manner. Various sketches of scenes would be laid out on a giant board and the animators came together and had story meetings, filling in the gaps, rejecting what didn't work.

A mind map is a highly effective way of addressing a situation, planning a strategy for new growth, or introducing new products. It's also an exceptional tool for helping you reach goals and make your dreams come true.

An Example of Using a Mind Map to Build Your Own Independent Business

People all over the world, in all walks of life, are building their own independent businesses to reach their goals and realize their dreams. In the following mind map, this person chose to start their own business.

Map Out the Elements of Building Your Business or Profession

Now take out your action plan with the descriptions of your activities and the one, three and five year statements. Here's what you need to make your mind map:

♦ A large piece of paper—either white or brown Kraft paper or construction paper—some people even like to use graph paper. (If you hang your map on a wall as you develop it, put up two layers of paper so the markers don't bleed through to your wall.)

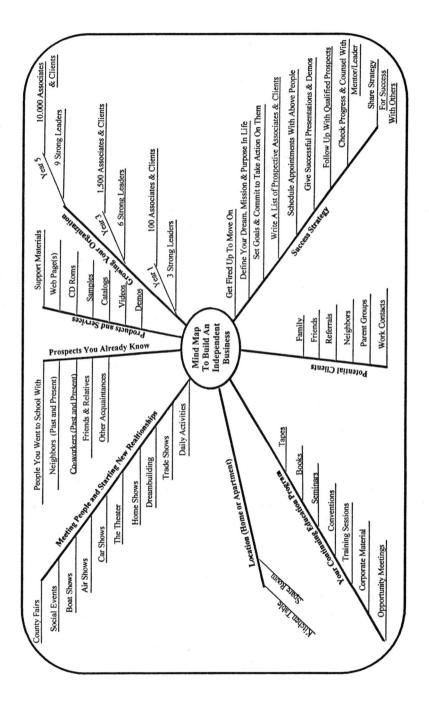

♦ Colorful felt-tip *non-permanent* markers. Make each major branch a different color and, in some cases, you may want to draw in pictures rather than write words.
♦ A notebook for recording your ideas and thoughts later.
♦ Artists' white tape or masking tape.
♦ Your action plan for building your business/profession.
♦ At least half an hour alone in a quiet place.

Once you have all your tools assembled, look at your action plan, especially the one, three, and five year statements. As you read them, you'll probably get ideas about what needs to happen so you can reach your goals.

Start drawing different branches, and label them with your ideas, which will bring them to life on your page. It's fine if it's busy and crowded—this is strictly for you. Brainstorm as many sub-branches as you can, remembering to group them under major branches wherever possible.

Ask Yourself These Questions

Here are some questions that may stimulate you to think of ideas for new branches. (There may be a couple of questions that aren't relevant to your action plan—depending on what it is. If that's the case, just ignore those particular questions.)

♦ *What resources or skills* do I need for my action plan?
♦ *Where* do I want to do my action plan?
♦ *Who* do I need to contact to make my action plan happen?
♦ *How* can I reach my one, three, and five-year goals?
♦ *What information* do I need?
♦ *How much money* do I need to start my action plan?
♦ Who do I know who is successful in my industry that I could ask for business/professional counseling and support?
♦ *What else* do I need to make my action plan happen?
♦ What kind of *help* might I need from my family?

♦ *Who benefits* from my action plan?
♦ What *needs to change* i.e., be given a different priority, or perhaps be eliminated from my life for me to implement my action plan?

Be Open to the Wealth of Infinite Possibilities

Now that you have a preliminary mind map, you can develop it even more to gain greater insight. Sit down and share it with your mentor or leader. This is the best way to get valuable advice and suggestions, based on your current situation and what's happening in your business or profession. Sharing your mind map is exciting and makes your action plan seem more real.

The mind map is a place to collect ideas as a strategic tool. It doesn't represent a commitment, so allow yourself to be spontaneous as possible when creating it. The time for decisions and commitments is later. This is the time to have fun—*let your imagination run free.*

Keep in mind the words of William James, "Man alone, of all the creatures of earth, can change his pattern. Man alone is architect of his destiny...."

Now Take These *Are You Fired Up?* Action Steps

♦ If you have not done so already, create your mind map.
♦ Be sure to ask yourself the questions in this chapter.
♦ After you've created your mind map, talk with your leader or mentor and ask them to contribute ideas. Add their ideas to your mind map and watch it grow.

Chapter 11

Make the Most of Your Resources

Build Your Fire Right Where You Are

"Taking advantage of the information and tools that are already available to you is a smart thing to do."

Are You Fired Up? **Principle #13—***Use Your Resources*

Webster's Dictionary defines resource as—"a reserve supply of support; something to which one has recourse in difficulty; an ability to meet and handle a situation." They can be tangible, like books and tapes, or intangible, as peace of mind and happiness. Ranging from legal and financial to educational, spiritual, motivational, and others, resources are essential to helping you achieve your dreams.

In July 1996, U.S. Olympic gymnast Kerri Strug made history as she led the women's team to victory. A quiet and barely visible team member until then, she had worked hard to get there. Changing coaches over the years, she finished seventh in the 1995 World Championships in Japan. But she was confused and fearful at that event, and in need of support. She returned to the rugged training of Bela Karolyi, knowing she'd be second in importance to another gymnast. Kerri's disposition was what concerned her coach the most.

Frequently injured and generally high strung, she often had difficulty sleeping.

After rigorous training with Karolyi and an emphasis on *team first*, Kerri led the U.S. team through the first two days of the Olympic competition with excellence. Then came the deciding event. Another female gymnast failed at both vault attempts. Even though Kerri had injured herself on her first vault, she knew the only way the team could win the gold medal was to do the second vault.

Cheered on by Karolyi, Kerri prayed for help and charged down the runway for an outstanding vault performance. She couldn't even stand up after she was done; her ankle was sprained so badly. But she had done it—she had won the gold medal for her team and her country, and her life would never be the same again.

None of Kerri's success could have occurred without substantial resources. Her coach, team members and family were people resources. Funding for her trips enabled her to go get the training she needed. And in those last few moments, she turned to God for the inner strength to carry on and triumph. No one, no matter how famous or wealthy, can make their dreams come true without utilizing resources.

As you get fired up about your dream, you may find you need several resources to achieve it. You may not even be aware of exactly which resources you currently have and which ones you need to develop. On the following page is an example of a resource list for starting your own independent business. Divided into 11 categories, there are specific resources suggested, and there could be some other resources under each one of those. This list is just an example and isn't meant to be official or comprehensive.

For example, a married couple who owned a farm decided they needed to change their lifestyle and started their own independent business.

RESOURCE LIST FOR STARTING YOUR OWN INDEPENDENT BUSINESS

BUSINESS OWNERSHIP PLAN

-RELATIONSHIPS
-PRESENTATION SUPPLIES
-PROSPECTING TOOLS
-SAMPLE PRODUCTS
-CATALOGS/BROCHURES
-WEB SITE(S)/CD ROM(S)

LEGAL

-SUPPLIER CORP. BYLAWS
AND RULES OF CONDUCT

FINANCIAL

-START UP COSTS
-CHECKBOOK

LOCATION/SUPPLIES

-HOME OFFICE/KITCHEN TABLE
-OFFICE EQUIPMENT/SUPPLIES
  -BOOKS AND TAPES
-COMPUTER

INDUSTRY SPECIFIC

-LEADER OR MENTOR
-SEMINARS
-PRODUCT FAIRS
-CONVENTIONS
-PUBLICATIONS

EDUCATION & TRAINING

-ONE-ON-ONE COUNSELING
-BOOKS, TAPES AND VIDEOS
-SEMINARS AND CONVENTIONS
-TRAINING SESSIONS
-OTHER LEADERSHIP EVENTS

PERSONAL SUPPORT STRUCTURE

-MENTOR OR LEADER
-POSITIVE THINKING FAMILY
AND FRIENDS
-BUSINESS ASSOCIATES

MOTIVATION & INSPIRATION

-BOOKS, TAPES & VIDEOS
-SEMINARS & CONVENTIONS
-DREAMBUILDING SESSIONS
-TRAINING SESSIONS AND OTHER
LEADERSHIP EVENTS

TIME/ACTIVITY MANAGEMENT

-PLANNER/DATEBOOK
-BALANCING HOME, WORK
& BUSINESS
-GOAL SETTING, PLANNING &
SCHEDULING

HEALTH (PHYSICAL & MENTAL)

-DIET & NUTRITION
-VITAMINS & SUPPLEMENTS
-EXERCISE
-REST

SPIRITUAL

- INSPIRATIONAL READING
- PRAYER

They needed only a minimum of financial resources for the following: start-up items and optional tools; education—to get the right training in people skills and leadership development; and prospecting—to help them bring people into their organization to be independent business owners, as well as to find others to be members and clients. They didn't need any employees or manufacturing facilities. Instead, they found the business they choose to be fairly simple.

Are You Fired Up? **Principle #14—***Connect with the Right People*

Whenever you begin something like going for a new dream, you need to know your resources. It would be naïve of us to think we could do everything alone. However, again, we don't need to "reinvent the wheel." We can learn from those who are where we want to be. Duplicating their pattern of success can help us succeed.

Taking advantage of the information and tools already available to you is a smart thing to do. You may not know where the answer to one of your challenges will come from; you may not know who has the contact that will lead you to the next leader in your business or profession. It has been said that we are all, at most, just seven people away from anyone in the world. It would take only seven contacts to reach the president of a country or well-known chief executive officer, or anyone else.

The key is to make a list of people you can contact and start taking action. You may be better connected than you believe you are. Statistics show that, on average, most people know about 250 other people. People are the greatest resources. People are first; products and services follow. You just need to go through the noes to connect with the right people who agree with you and have a vision for their future.

As you meet people and make new friends, remember what Dale Carnegie said· "You can make more friends in two months by becoming more interested in others than you can in two years by trying to get them interested in you."

Sometimes the best way others can help you is to believe in you and your ability to achieve your dreams. And in any quest, your leader or mentor shows you they believe in you by supporting your efforts to build your business or profession. You can then pass this belief on to others and help them achieve their dreams. From a tiny spark, the flames of enthusiasm can spread very quickly.

Contrary to popular belief, no one is self-made. It takes the cooperation of other people to realize a big dream. No one can become successful alone, no matter what field of endeavor they may choose. And the best way anyone can succeed is to help others succeed. Be committed to helping others, and good things will happen in your life.

Use the *Are You Fired Up?* Action Plan with Resources

You're now ready to focus on the action plan for your dream. Spend about ten minutes reviewing which resources you may already have (like motivation and contacts) and which resources you may need to develop (perhaps a clearer vision of what you want, a relationship with your leader or mentor, and time/activity management).

What specific results would you like to see from this dream? You may want to retire from your job or current business to work your new business full-time. What strengths do you still need to build to be successful? Maybe you need to learn to ignore negative thinking people who are trying to steal your dream. Carefully consider each of your answers. They will be useful in helping you decide which action steps to take next, so you can make progress on your dream.

You may still need several resources. Do whatever it takes to get what you need to build your business or profession so you can make your dreams come true. Take advantage of your industry's system of success and encourage your associates to do the same.

You're investing in yourself and remember, when you are passionate, committed, and fired up, people will come into your life who believe in what you're doing. By helping them achieve their dreams you can achieve yours too. It is a well known fact of success that the more people you help achieve what they want, the more you'll achieve as well. It's simply impossible to be successful alone.

When you have a big enough dream, no matter how many obstacles you have, you can overcome them.

Strengths That Need to Be Developed for This Dream:

1._____

2._____

3._____

Resources I Have: **Resources I Need:**

1.   1.

2.   2.

3.   3.

Now Take These *Are You Fired Up?* Action Steps

- ♦ If you haven't already done so, read over the resources lists and determine those which you already have and those you need to develop. Complete that section of the Action Plan on the previous page.
- ♦ Review your mind map from earlier in the book to see what other resources you have and which ones you need. Add these to your Action Plan.

Chapter 12

What About Money?

Keep a Constant Supply of Kindling

"We believe that getting our finances in order—paying off our debts, learning to share with others, setting financial limits and faithfully living within them—is the beginning of getting our lives to move forward."
Rich DeVos

Persist and Reap the Rewards

Many people use their creativity to develop financial resources when working on their dreams. Some people even sell household items, like a television, to get the money they need to move on. On the other hand, many others use their lack of financial resources as an excuse not to do something. How about you? Do you have the attitude that nothing is going to get in the way of achieving your dream? That's what champions believe. They do whatever it takes.

The United States is the wealthiest country in the world, yet there are still homeless, starving people on the streets. While most people are gainfully employed, they still operate from a philosophy of not having enough. This poverty thinking is fueled by debt and the obsession with credit card spending. This level of thinking has a built-in negative belief system that says, "There is not enough for everyone, therefore there is not enough for me." This is a limiting belief and it is false. It is very different from wealth thinking which says there is more than enough for all of us, and that we are all capable of enjoying and sharing in it. Be sure you are thinking wealth rather than poverty; it can make a big difference in how easily you achieve your dreams. As former U.S. President Harry S. Truman once said, "There is enough in the world for everyone to have plenty to live on happily and to be at peace with his neighbors."

Fortunately, there are excellent books and techniques to help change a poverty focus to one of wealth and freedom. There are a number of books available that have effective suggestions and tools for overcoming debt and cultivating wealth in all areas of your life. It is absolutely essential for you to get out of debt and live within your means so you can build your wealth. Check with your leader or mentor and ask what books they might recommend for you to read.

When you realize that wealth is so much more than money, you'll get fired up about how truly wealthy you already are. When you are grateful for all the blessings you already have in your life, it increases your possibilities of receiving more. Always have an attitude of gratitude.

Are You Fired Up? **Principle #15—***Manage Your Money and Get Out of Debt*

Another reason why people sometimes struggle financially is they feel *unworthy* of success or wealth. Again, myths from earlier in life can hold you back today—*but only if you let them.* It is time to uncover and let go of these myths, like you did in Chapter 6. Often such myths are deeply ingrained in the subconscious and they have a powerful hold on people—until they let them go.

One way to tell if you need to uncover more myths is to notice where you may be stuck. Ask yourself, "What have I been striving to do financially where I've been repeatedly unsuccessful? What is it I believe that may be false and holding me back from achieving my goals?"

I used to think that if I owned a beautiful home, I wouldn't ever get married. And I really wanted to be happily married. After I recognized this myth, I let it go and built a beautiful house on the river. It started just as a slab of concrete. Week after week I watched it grow into a lovely home, which became my tranquil refuge. A year and a half after I moved in, I met my husband, who "fell in love" with the house soon after he fell in love with me!

To uncover any money myths that may be holding you back from fully achieving your dreams and the success you want, spend a few minutes on the following activity.

Money Myths Activity

Get a tape recorder with a blank tape and give yourself 15 minutes alone in a quiet place. Turn the recorder on and just start freely talking about money. Start with statements like "Money is...," or "I think money is...," or "From the viewpoint of my father money is...," "From the viewpoint of my mother, money is...," "In the eyes of my religion, money is...," "From the perspective of my business or profession, money is...," and let yourself ramble on. Pour out any thoughts which come to mind about money. After you are through, take a break.

Come back in a half-hour, with a pen and paper, and listen to what you said. Notice any limiting beliefs you have about money.

For instance, many people mistakenly believe that the Bible says that "money is the root of all evil." But what it really says is that "the *love* of money is *a* root of evil." Money *is just a tool*—a medium of exchange—and it is neutral. It is neither good nor bad. It is compensation for services rendered. It is used to do good things in the hands of good people. And it's the only thing that can do what it does.

It builds churches, schools, hospitals, colleges, universities, and other public buildings. It puts a roof over your head, clothes on your back, and food on your table.

List all the myths and study them. You may discover something that has prevented you from enjoying greater wealth up until now. Then, draw an "X" through the page, erase the tape and tear up the paper as a symbol of your letting go of those myths. With your new awareness, they won't hold you back any more. Congratulations! You have just created an "open space" in your mind to receive wealth inducing ideas. Nature abhors a vacuum—give it a vacuum to fill! Fill your mind with ideas that will support you in your quest to achieve your financial goals.

Here are a few key ideas to help you increase your wealth relative to monthly spending and credit card usage. Let these get you fired up about getting rid of debt and building your wealth.

Tip #1—*Credit Cards*

Credit cards are recommended as a convenience. In fact, many people prefer to carry them instead of cash. Just endeavor to pay off the balance each month to avoid paying interest. A helpful technique is to *write down every credit card purchase in your checkbook and subtract it from the balance.* Put a little box or star around it so you know it's a credit card expense and not a check. Then when the bill comes in, you already have the money set aside to pay for these purchases. You are not increasing your debt or incurring any finance charges, and you start each month with a zero credit card balance.

Tip #2—*Debit Cards*

You may want to use a debit card, which automatically withdraws cash directly from your checking account as you spend it. This is a safer method than a credit card because you can only spend what you have in the bank. You can get a debit card from your bank, and they operate just like a check. It helps to record the amount you spend with your debit card in your day planner. Enter it on the date you spend it. Put it in a separate section of your planner, if you don't have your checkbook with you. But remember to record your usage in your checkbook, so you always know how much money is in your account. This kind of card comes in handy when ordering flowers or deliveries over the phone—times when a check may not work.

Tip #3—*Lower Interest Rates and No Annual Fees*

There are many ways to *cut down on credit card interest and eliminate annual fees as you pay off any credit card debt* you may have. Interest rates and annual fee practices vary a great deal from bank to bank. Most people don't question these costs, not realizing that this mistake could cost them hundreds, and possibly even thousands, of dollars.

If you live in the U.S., you may want to check out "Bankcard Holders of America (BHA)." They describe themselves as "A non-profit organization helping bankcard holders become informed consumers." If you live outside the U.S., you may want to inquire at your bank about the availability of a similar organization where you live. BHA offers a "Low-Interest/No-Fee Credit Card List" for $4. You can write to them at 524 Branch Drive, Salem, VA 24153. Be sure to enclose your check for $4 (mailing cash isn't recommended).

I once had an experience with this myself, which may benefit you. One of my credit cards had increased my line of credit by $4000 at a low interest rate. I called to verify that this was not a short-term trick offer and then I asked, "If I use the increased credit line to pay off other credit cards what would my rate be?" Their credit division reviewed my excellent credit history and permanently lowered the interest rate on the entire balance on the card, including the new

$4000 line. Delighted, I decided to get my other card rates lowered, too. Fifty percent of them did, in fact, lower my rate, which ended up saving me hundreds of dollars in interest.

You can do it, too. Ask to speak to someone in customer service and tell them what you want to do. Also check if you can get a better interest rate by agreeing to shift all your credit card debt and other banking business to the bank with the lowest interest rates. You'll be happy to discover that you can often lower your interest rate just by asking! In the process, you could also ask them to waive any annual fee. Keep asking for what you want.

Tip #4—*Freezer Fix*

If you go shopping, leave all your credit cards at home, so you won't be tempted to spend money you don't have. Also, avoid television shopping. You can impulsively spend lots of money on things you really don't need by getting caught up in an infomercial or home shopping show. Another idea is to take all your credit cards and freeze them in an ice block, so it's difficult to use them. Or you could even keep the credit card with the best interest rate, and cut the rest up and throw them away!

Tip #5—*Consolidation Loans*—Buyer Beware

It's likely you've seen finance companies' advertisements that promise to consolidate your debt into one loan, at less interest and smaller monthly payments. They often try to make their offer seem even more attractive by lending you *more* money than you need.

Two things generally result when people borrow from such companies: 1)They borrow more money and get even deeper in debt for a longer period of time. 2)With their new "paid off" credit cards, instead of closing the accounts, they continue their charging habit. They often charge until they load up again to their credit limit.

So not only are these people not better because of their consolidation loan, they're usually worse off! They could jeopardize their families to the point they may lose everything and even go bankrupt.

Be very suspect of those "too good to be true" sounding ads. They usually are! A well thought-out plan to pay off those credit card accounts and your other loans too, is a better bet. For example, get all your credit card debt onto one or two cards with the lowest interest rates. Also look for cards with the lowest or no annual fees, and pay off more than the minimum each month.

Becoming debt-free is one of the best goals you can have. Debt drains your energy and drags you down. Having no debt frees you up and gets you fired up. Keep persisting until you pay your credit card debt off and eliminate credit card interest altogether. It's worth it!

Now Take These *Are You Fired Up?* Action Steps

♦ If you have not already done so, do the money myths activity in this chapter.

♦ Review your financial situation. Record all your debts, assets and resources. Make a goal of becoming debt-free and financially free.

♦ Do your best to calculate exactly what you need financially for your dream. Talk with your leader or mentor and ask for their recommendations.

♦ Stay on track; follow a proven system of success so you can make it happen for you.

Chapter 13

Make Each Day Count

Fanning the Flames

*"Make it a point to do something every day that you don't
want to do. This is the golden rule for acquiring the habit of doing
what we need to do without pain."*
Mark Twain

Are You Fired Up? Principle #16—*Use Your Time Wisely*

As you stay fired up about your dream, you'll soon
discover that one of the best ways to support yourself is
through effective time/activity management. You may have
already taken an excellent time management course before,
for example like Franklin Covey offers. Here's a new
perspective for you to consider as you build your business or
profession and balance your other priorities, too.

Bestselling author and speaker, Stephen Covey shares an
interesting story which goes like this:

In a lecture one time, the instructor said, "We're now
going to have a quiz." He pulled out a wide-mouth gallon jar
and several large fist-size rocks. He asked the class, "How
many of these rocks do you think we can get into the jar?"
After many guesses from his students, he began to stuff the
rocks into the jar until no more rocks would fit. He then
asked, "Is the jar full?" The class responded, "Yes." The
instructor then said, "Aah—wait," and took a bucket of

gravel and dumped it into the jar. The gravel filled some of the spaces left by the big rocks. He then asked again, "Is the jar full?" By this time the class was beginning to understand the lesson he was teaching them. "Probably not," they replied. "Good," the instructor said, and he brought out a bucket of sand. He dumped the sand into the jar, and it began to fill all the crevices left by the large rock and the gravel. He asked again, "Is the jar full?" "No!" said the class enthusiastically. He then took a quart of water and poured it into the jar, completely saturating all the little crevices between the sand, gravel and rocks. "The point is," he said, "that if you had not put the big rocks in first, you would never have gotten any of them into the jar."

Many people try to stuff way too much "sand, gravel, and water" into their lives without investing time to schedule in the "big rocks." The big rocks represent the most significant things in your life, the ones which give your life happiness, meaning and substance. In Chapter 7, you examined what your values are and what is truly most meaningful to you. In the next activity, you'll have the opportunity to refine your list even more, by identifying and focusing on your top priorities. This activity is very worthwhile, because once you know what your big rocks are, you can set up your entire time management program around what is really most important to you. It means *you* are in control—*not* the outside world. Consciously making your own choices helps you to be fired up about your life. This is key.

"Big Rocks" Activity

Get out a piece of paper and take a few minutes now to make a quick list of those things in your life that are most important to you. Don't worry about the order you put them in, just quickly jot them down as they come to mind. Here are some examples—*spiritual life, spouse, children, dream, job, business, health.*

Once you have listed them go back and rank them in their order of priority in your life. Now you know what items you need to put on your calendar and in your date book, day planner or appointment book first. Look over what you've got going next week and schedule in time for each of the big rocks listed above, giving special priority to rocks 1-5.When you schedule your big rocks first, you will attend to the most important things in your life, and you will feel happier, more fulfilled and fired up. This is a significantly different approach than most time planning systems, which have you scheduling according to critical deadlines and other people's agendas.

Compromises may be necessary—especially if you work for someone else. But it's much easier to talk to your boss about other options, rather than working late on a particular night, if you have already written a prior commitment in your planner. You can say something like this to your boss as way of explanation: "I'm busy tonight after work. If I had known about this sooner, I would have rearranged my schedule. However, I'll be happy to come in early or stay late tomorrow. Would that be okay with you?" Most of the time bosses accept that approach, as long as your request is clear and reasonable. They're also likely to respect you more because you are showing respect for yourself and your family. Yet you are doing it in an inoffensive way, intent on making it a win-win situation.

So, in addition to using the big rock approach, *how else can you use your time better?* Here are five tips to help you stay fired up and on target with your dream.

Time Tip #1—*Use a Time/Activity Management System*

Get yourself an excellent time/activity management system, like the Franklin Planner®, which is more comprehensive than an appointment book. You'll want a system that has at least one full page for each day (the

Franklin has two), and it's best if it's loose-leaf in format so that you can put pages in and around your daily sheets. It's best to take your planner everywhere you go. Whenever you have a thought about something which needs to be done, you can record it in the appropriate place. Otherwise, you are likely to have a lot of floating pieces of paper which are subject to getting lost!

Several years back, I took a sales course. We were given a test to measure our sales abilities. I did well on the test, except for one area—time/activity management. The instructor emphasized how important it is to get a good time/activity management system to track everything you are doing and record all your creative ideas. That convinced me to get a system. Make sure you use your system regularly and choose the color and size that really appeals to you. Many people feel more successful when they use one of these systems. That, alone, is a great benefit!

Time Tip #2—*Using Your Planner*

First of all, set up your planner so you have only three months of dated days in it; this month, last month and next month. There's usually a convenient plastic ruler which comes with it that helps you easily turn to today's date. After next month's dated days, have a section for months, where you keep the two-page miniature calendars for the next 12 months of the year. You can write down future commitments and agreements in your planner. Remember, broken agreements destroy relationships and damage your self-esteem. *Keep your promises to yourself and others* by writing them all down and then taking appropriate action.

Now, have several sections in the back with dividers for your "big rocks." You would label each accordingly and put in any pertinent information in them. Things like personal and family dream lists, prospect and customer lists, sizes, birthdates and other key information fit in the back section.

Also be sure to have a section for your dream. And put in any relevant paperwork there, like your mind map and action plan. (By the way, the Classic Franklin Planner has pages that are 6" wide x 8" long. To make an 8½" x 11" sheet fit into the Classic Franklin Planner, reduce it to 65 percent of its size.) In the back, record all of your addresses and phone numbers, including both business and personal, so they are handy to you at all times.

Also be sure to *include a miniature Feel Good Folder in your planner,* which holds pictures of your loved ones, and letters and cards from others. They'll make you feel good when you see them. You can turn to these items when you have a challenging day and instantly feel more positive. Use the zipper-type sections to hold your feel-good items.

One thing that might be going through your mind is, "What happens if I lose my planner?" The answer is, don't! You will find it to be such a valuable tool that you will want to keep it with you all the time. However, be sure to put your name, address and phone number in the front, so it can be returned to you—just in case.

My husband lost his planner a few years ago on Christmas Eve. He left it in a shopping cart at a grocery store parking lot. By the time he got home, he realized it was missing. He went back to the store, but the book was gone. He wanted to order one that night to replace it. I told him to wait—it was Christmas Eve and I was certain someone would return it to him. Sure enough, later that night, the local post office called and said someone had turned it in there. A postman delivered it to us on Christmas morning! Talk about service.

Time Tip #3—*No More "To Do" Lists*

Here's a question for you. How often do you get to the end of the day and discover there are still things to do on your to do list? When I asked seminar groups this question, almost everyone raises their hand. How does that feel? Not very good. It's best to write down and prioritize only what you can reasonably expect to do in a day. Allow time for unexpected challenges. Then, as you check off what you have done that day, you can feel positive about it. You can choose to move anything undone to another day or decide you're not going to do it at all, for whatever reason.

To keep yourself on track with your business or profession, you need to write down the dates and times of meetings, seminars, and other special events you need to attend. The easiest thing to do is put these in the monthly calendar at the start of each month and as needed. Do this as soon as you become aware of places you need to go and things you need to do. Reschedule anything you must—to take full advantage of whatever activities will help you move ahead. This is one of the most important ways you can stay focused and fired up to make your dreams come true. You'll also be a good example to others as you grow in your leadership ability and responsibilities.

Time Tip #4—*Write Down Daily Success Lists*

Another tool is the daily success list. Use one of the sections in the back of your planner. If you don't have a planner yet, use a notebook or get yourself one of those attractive books with blank pages in it. At the end of each day, write down at least ten successes you had that day.

Some people may judge themselves negatively and say they had no success. But realize that every positive action you take, no matter how small, is considered a success because you did something. Movement is the key. Every phone call you made to a prospect, customer, or client, is a success, regardless of how they responded. Every time you made a presentation is a success, whether they're interested or not. Whether you get the outcome you want or not, you have taken positive action and such action is always rewarded in some way. In some cases the reward is that you learned something valuable you can use later—like what *not* to do! Or perhaps you did something you were afraid to do and you have increased your confidence as a result. Regardless of what happens, you want to keep going because it will help you stay fired up. If you don't take action, you'll frustrate yourself because you won't get the results you say you want. Successful people persist until they reach their goal—they don't give up.

For instance, many successful business people believe that for every ten noes they receive, they get one yes. In fact, they actually thank the no people enthusiastically, because they figure that puts them one step closer to a yes. They understand that following their industry's success system, while continually taking action doing whatever it takes, is key to growing their business or profession.

Some of the things you are working on may still be in progress, but you took the necessary action today and that is a win. (For example, you've scheduled some business presentations but haven't called yet to confirm them.) Let's face it, some days just getting out of bed and going to work is a success, particularly if you didn't feel like it. *Tracking your success consistently gives you an incredible boost to your self-esteem.* You know you're making progress.

I had a wonderful experience with this in a course I once took. Part of our weekly assignment was to record our successes. I was really surprised at what a difference it made. I did it for about 300 days that year, and when I looked back at the book at the end of the year, I saw how much I had accomplished. It said to me, "You are a person who gets things done. You are successful and effective." I was fired up about my ability to achieve. I know it may seem silly, but it works. Do it for at least two months and see for yourself. When you look back over all that you have done, you'll probably find that you do a great deal and you are a winner.

Time Tip #5—*Live in the Present*

Far too many people make the mistake of spending their time worrying about things that have happened or could happen. Or they are often mentally reliving the "good old days," or projecting their lives too far in the future. In the process, they miss the present! Truly successful people know that the only real time we have is now, so they make the most of each moment. When you're living in the present, you're in your most resourceful and productive state. In fact, it's the only time you can take action!

While you keep a vision of your dream and your future in front of you, do what you can today and enjoy the experience of appreciating and living in the present. Forget yesterday; it's over and gone. Focus on what you can do right now in this very moment. Each minute counts. Use them to progressively reach your goals and dreams. You'll be happy you did!

By fully living every moment in the present, you can take action, get results and triumph. Be fired up in the present with your creative imagination, and your dream will become much more alive and attainable.

Now Take These *Are You Fired Up?* Action Steps

♦ When you are ready, invest in a day planner for yourself in the color and size you'd like. It'll help you stay organized and fired up.

♦ When you're ready, invest in a new system which looks great and helps you stay organized and fired up. Then set it up as suggested in Time Tips 2 & 3. Use it every day and always keep it with you.

Chapter 14

Upgrade Your Vitality

Breathe Life into the Fire

"Developing healthy habits is simple and essential to our success. We need the stamina to achieve our goals and dreams, and the good health to enjoy the new life we've created."

Are You Fired Up? **Principle # 17—*Take Care of Your Health***

Be aware that your physical and mental health are important resources to living your dreams. Feeling good physically and mentally helps keep you fired up about life and your dream. Sadly, health is a resource many people tend to overlook.

I witnessed how poor health can destroy your life through my mother's long-term illness and subsequent death. I saw a brilliant, artistic, beautiful woman disintegrate into a jaundiced, frail shell of a human being, in constant pain. After 15 years in and out of the hospital, she finally died at 45. Her illness and death colored my life and health choices significantly. As I have aged, I have learned to take good care of myself. That starts first with a healthy, balanced diet, followed by regular, fun exercise and relaxation. I prefer to be as natural in my approach to health as possible. Here's five tips for living healthy.

Health Tip #1—*Take Vitamins, Minerals, and Antioxidants*

Certainly, a well-balanced diet is the best source of excellent nutrition, but because of extensive food processing, the next best sources are vitamins, minerals, antioxidants, and other supplements. Read about them and do what is best for your health. Invest in yourself.

Health Tip #2—*Exercise Four to Five Times a Week*

The latest research shows that 30 minutes of exercising which gets your heart rate up and you enjoy four times a week, can add years to your life. Find an activity, like brisk walking, that you can do wherever you are. All you need is comfortable sneakers or walking shoes.

You could even listen to audiotapes as you walk and get both physically and mentally fired up at the same time. You could also do some stretching and toning exercises with light weights, sit-ups, and leg lifts. Be sure to consult with your physician before you embark on any exercise program.

Health Tip #3—*Eat Four to Five Fruits and Vegetables a Day*

The various diet and nutrition books on the market all suggest to eat lots of fruits and vegetables, while cutting down on sugar, fat and salt. It's easy to work four or five servings of fruits, and vegetables into your day, when you plan it by including juice, fruits and raw vegetables like carrots as snacks.

Health Tip #4—*Drink Lots of Water*

This is another tip most of us have heard for a long time, but now more than ever, it's important to drink plenty of water to keep you fit and fired up. Drink at least 8 glasses of water every day. Water fills you up, flushes out toxins and can help your skin be more elastic and younger looking. You might also want to add a water treatment system for your drinking water. It'll save you money in the long-run over buying bottled water.

Health Tip #5—*Get Enough Rest*

Daily sleep requirements vary. You need less when you're fired up about your dream, eat properly, exercise and take food supplements. When you're running hard for a goal and sleep less than normal, a 30-minute nap in the late afternoon or early evening can help.

Before you fall asleep and when you wake up, focus on your dream. Your mind is more relaxed and receptive right before you go to sleep and when you first awake, making it easier for your subconscious to work on it. It is like planting a seed in fertile soil which helps you stay fired up, focused and on track. Putting dreambuilding pictures on the wall by your bed helps with this process.

Are You Fired Up? **Principle # 18 — *Laugh about It!***

One of the most powerful ingredients for health is laughter. Take yourself lightly and life seriously, and laugh at your own mistakes. This helps you to take your challenges in stride and to keep a positive attitude. Buy a clean joke or riddle book. Take the book with you or write down some of the jokes and riddles and share them with others.

Also, look for the humor in everyday events. Have you ever had the experience of pure fun and laughter when you're among family, friends and associates? Have you ever felt the freeing feeling of a very deep belly laugh? That laughter releases endorphins into your body and makes you feel good. Laughter helps you to relax your system and gets the energy flowing inside you. It gets you fired up.

Are You Fired Up? **Principle # 19—***Dreams Help Keep You Alive and Excited about Life*

Another factor in recovering from illness or injury is the power of dreams. *When you have dreams to live for, you can overcome almost any health challenge.* That is certainly true for countless athletes who have triumphed over serious injuries.

In 1983 Joan Benoit, renowned Olympic marathon runner, had surgery done on both Achilles tendons.   Seemingly recovered, she began preparing for the 1984 Olympics. Only two months before the trials, she had severe pain in her right knee, which slowed down her running. For a while, her doctor injected cortisone into her knees. But the pain returned to such an extent that she could barely walk.

Courageously, Benoit took a major risk. With only 17 days to go before the Olympic trials, she underwent orthoscopic surgery. Afterwards, she felt no pain. But later, she overcompensated with her left leg, hurting her hamstring. After her initial uncertainty, she decided to start the trials and see how far she could go. Not only did she make the trials, she excelled. On August 5, 1984, she led the pack of runners on a 26-mile Olympic marathon. She made medical and sports history and took the gold medal. Her dream got her fired up and led her to victory.

Take care of your health. Get and keep your body as sound as possible and have a positive attitude. This will support you as you go for your dreams. Having vitality and a great attitude makes it easier to do whatever it takes to stay fired up and make your dreams come true. Focusing on good health is a great way to do that. Do the best you can with what you have in this area. If you have a major physical or mental challenge, you can still take good care or yourself, rouse your enthusiasm and move on to a better life. As someone wise once said, "In every adversity there is a seed of equal or greater benefit." You can do it too!

Now Take These *Are You Fired Up?* Action Steps

- Check with your doctor to find out what he or she recommends for improving your health.
- Schedule a regular exercise program into your planner, and stick to it.
- Rent or borrow some movies which you find funny from comedians you like, such as Bill Cosby and Robin Williams.
- See what vitamins, minerals, antioxidants and other supplements you could take. Invest in yourself.
- Consider purchasing a water treatment system. It'll be worth it and will save you money over buying bottled water.

Chapter 15

A Positive Attitude Is Essential

Rekindle the Fire Inside of You

"Every great and commanding movement in the annals of the world is the triumph of enthusiasm. Nothing great was ever achieved without it."
Ralph Waldo Emerson

How Is Your Attitude?

In 1914 Thomas Edison, one of the world's great thinkers, faced a very difficult challenge. His laboratory and all the work inside it caught fire and burned to the ground. Instead of being dismayed and quitting, like so many people would have done, he said, "All the mistakes are burned up. Thank God we can start anew." That's the mark of a true optimist; one who faces the world with a positive perspective, no matter what. Having a positive attitude is essential in maintaining enthusiasm for your dream and staying fired up.

Are You an Optimist?

Your attitude is completely within your control. In fact, it is one of the few things that is. Best-selling author and speaker, Alan Loy McGinnis concludes, after studying the lives of thousands of successful people: "The road to a happy and successful life is paved with optimism." That's not to say life won't provide you with challenges nor that you should ignore the difficulties that present themselves along the way. Inside each challenge is a solution and a lesson. Understand that, *what happens to you happens for you.* Always look for the good in everything and *grow through* the experience.

It's easy to be positive when things are going well. But when you encounter an obstacle—now *that's* where the true test of your attitude comes in! How you view and handle a particular situation is your choice; you can become negative and pessimistic and just complain, or you can look for the solutions and draw on your available resources. Each situation is just an opportunity in disguise to learn and grow—a chance to become the best you can be. In overcoming the obstacle you gain the strength you need to continue.

Growing in a Foreign Country

I certainly know how important attitude is in my life. When I was 16, I went to live in Kingston, Jamaica with a Jamaican family I had met a few years earlier. I taught English as a volunteer for a month there, as part of my senior project in school.

Even though I had tutored throughout high school, I was not expecting these junior high school classes in Kingston to be so large. There were 45 students in one class, 65 in another. The classrooms were concrete three-sided rooms with an open wall to let the air in.

Their rigorous school discipline also surprised me. Hearing a loud noise one day, I rushed outside to see what was happening. I ran to break up what I thought was a fight between two students, only to find the children cheering as a teacher was beating a boy who had been unruly. I was shocked. In the early 1970's Jamaican schools still maintained the British tradition of corporal punishment. That day lead to a turning point in my attitude. In spite of my fear, I decided to make a bigger difference in the lives of my students by teaching them self-discipline.

Fired up about my chance to make a contribution, I spent time with my students on a personal level. I took them on a field trip to the zoo *right next door;* something that had never been done! I got to know my students as people and learned that a lot of them never had money for lunch or even milk.

These children were bright and hungry to learn about the world; but many would never get beyond ninth grade. They would then go to work to support their families or become farmers. But they still wanted to reach out, so they became pen pals to my students in the United States.

My experience at this Jamaican school was very powerful. Many of the teachers there were optimistic and hopeful; they welcomed me and shared their stories with me. I learned that no matter what the system is or the rules are—*one person can make a difference and have a positive impact.*

I was so excited that I did my thesis on Jamaican education. I returned there several times while in college, and later, to do more research. I learned a great deal about myself and others, and grew wiser from my time there. I'm pleased to report Jamaican education has improved significantly since that time and there is more hope for the children there today.

As you move forward on you dream, you may find delays in the process, times when things don't go smoothly and doors don't get opened. That's the point at which you need to draw on your inner resources, keep having faith and rekindle your sparks inside. It's always an internal choice.

You never know what kind of good fortune will come out of adversity. At a minimum, you can learn and grow from it, making you stronger and more capable of handling future challenges. Hopefully, as you go along, your understanding and compassion for others will continue to deepen, so you can be an optimistic servant-leader of the finest caliber.

Julio Iglesias was a professional soccer player in Madrid, living that dream. One day he was severely hurt in a car crash and became paralyzed. He spent a long time in the hospital, and while there, a nurse gave him a guitar. Little did she know she would be launching the career of one of the world's most successful popular singers. What if Julio hadn't had the adversity of that car crash?

Are You Fired Up? Principle #20—*It Could Happen*

In the Disney film *Angels in the Outfield,* there's a young child, J.P., who lives in a foster home. His mother was homeless and had been raising him in the front seat of their car. In spite of his background, J.P. never gives up hope his mother will come back and take him home, or that some loving person will adopt him. His entire philosophy of life is summed up in his wistful phrase, which he repeats over and over to himself and others, *"It could happen."*

That line is key to the whole movie and to what happens to J.P. and Roger, the movie's main character, who also lives in the foster home. In the end, J.P. gets his wish—his dream comes true. A loving man and coach of the Angels baseball team happily adopts both of the two boys. The philosophy of *"It could happen,"* paid off.

Be open-minded. Realize you can follow in the footsteps of your leader or mentor. Once that door is open, all sorts of miracles can take place. So adopt a philosophy of possibility and realize that your dream *can* happen.

Are You Fired Up? Principle #21—*Remain Unattached to Outcomes*

One of the ways to help you get what you want is to *be unattached to the outcome,* while maintaining a positive focus and continuing to do whatever it takes. Some people want their dreams so badly that they push too hard and alienate others. They are so mentally attached to it that they actually prevent it from happening.

An example of this would be an overly aggressive salesperson who follows you around the car lot, not giving you a chance to think and sort out what you want. They hover over you and practically breathe down your neck. Most people would want to get away from such an anxious salesperson and probably never visit that lot again! Such people come across as desperate, trying to force an outcome which may be premature. This can drive others away! A wiser approach is to continue doing what you need to do to pursue your goal or dream, letting go of your desire to force it to happen, giving it some time and patience. If you go after someone—like a prospect or client—too aggressively, you can actually chase them away.

The attitude that you want to do whatever is best for them can help give them a sense of calm assurance. You're committed to your goal. But you are not attached to any particular person wanting to associate with you or buying your products and services. You know it will all work out because you are going to keep going until it does. You believe in everyone, but you depend on no one—but yourself.

Again, I know exactly how true this is because I have experienced it. In my early thirties, I really wanted to get married and share my life with a wonderful man. I *really, really* wanted it, so much so that I wanted to force it to happen. The men I dated apparently sensed my strong attachment to getting married and it probably scared them. That meant those relationships were, of course, short-lived.

After taking a personal growth seminar, I decided that I would be just fine, even if I spent the rest of my life alone. I no longer had to be married. I made it a preference, not an attachment. I was neutral, confident and open-minded. I continued to grow personally and be the best I could be. I had faith that whatever was supposed to happen would. Three short months later, my husband-to-be came to my office in need of an ad agency. Instead, he ended up with a wife who loves him very much, and no one was more surprised than me. Shortly after as I let go of the strong attachment to the outcome, the right man appeared!

Are You Fired Up? **Principle #22—*Be Patient***

Coupled right along with the concept of detachment is patience. I know that it can be difficult to be patient when you are working on your goals to make your dream come true. But, most dreams require a number of things to line up before you can make them happen. That means you need to have patience and faith as you are working through the process. As long as you are consistently taking appropriate action, good things will happen. Be aware that, as Henry Wadsworth Longfellow once said, "The heights by great men reached and kept were not attained by sudden flight. But they, while their companions slept, were toiling upward in the night."

Are You Fired Up? **Principle #23—*Learn from Your Mistakes***

Mary Lou Retton was the 1984 U.S. Olympic gold medalist in gymnastics who earned a perfect 10. She advises, *"Never ever give up on your dreams and don't be afraid to fail, because failure makes you a stronger person."*

Stay Fired Up with These Suggestions

So how do you use a positive attitude to stay fired up and keep going? Here are a few suggestions:

♦ *If you have a setback look for the lesson in it.* Ask yourself, "What can I learn from this experience?" Make notes about it.

♦ *Accept the setback.* Then picture it developing into a positive outcome. See it with perfect clarity as a victory, with the benefit yet to be realized.

♦ *Be careful how you describe each of your experiences.* It's better to consider failures as learning opportunities. This attitude will help you regard yourself in a positive way—knowing you aren't a failure, but rather a student of life, who is learning and growing. Be careful about the words you use; words create feelings. Support and encourage yourself. When you catch yourself in negative self-talk, say "Deflect" or "Cancel that." Keep negativity out of your thinking.

♦ *Ignore failure statistics.* Ignorance of negativity is bliss. In 1983 when I opened my business, four out of five small businesses failed nationally. If I had known that back then, I might never have started the business. Start taking action and do whatever it takes to make it happen.

♦ *Avoid negative thinking people.* They're the ones who are constantly complaining. They whine about everyone and everything—blaming everyone else for their difficulties. They're never happy for you when you succeed, because they're unhappy inside.

♦ *Seek a positive thinking mentor and role models.* Find a leader or mentor to counsel with about your business or profession. Associate with people who are more successful than you; people you can learn from and emulate. Duplicate their pattern of success. And keep in mind that, you can "associate" through books and tapes; it doesn't always have to be in person.

♦ *When you face a challenge, keep going.* Challenges are for you to *grow through*, not just go through. Fill out an action plan and do whatever it takes to keep going.

♦ *If you are stuck, get out of your inertia.* Do something constructive, just to get yourself moving. Whatever action you take, follow through with it until you finish the "assignment" you give yourself. Enjoy the feeling of accomplishment. This might mean meeting new people, calling a new prospect or client, dreambuilding, or getting together with your leader or mentor for support.

Do *something*, big or small. Take a positive action toward your dream. This helps you get back on track.

♦ *No matter how many situations you have to work through every day, focus on what you can do for others.* Build their dream, encourage them, to be a "good-finder," and help them achieve their goals and dreams. Each day ask yourself, *"How have I become a more loving person?"* and *"What have I learned to help me and others have a more positive attitude?"*

♦ *Be grateful.* In spite of your challenges, you have much to be thankful for. Without facing challenges and making mistakes, you won't receive the gifts of learning and growing. You're fortunate to have situations to deal with, which is how you learn and grow. As Helen Keller once said, *"The best way out is through."*

Are You Fired Up? Principle #24—*Cultivate an Attitude of Gratitude*

Make it a point to thank people for their assistance and support. Honor and appreciate others; it's part of being a caring person. For example, send handwritten thank you notes to your leader or mentor. Maybe a friend or family member babysat for you while you were out growing your profession or business. Do something special for those who help you. If your budget allows, you could send them balloons, a planter or flowers in addition to a note. You'll brighten their day and they'll be more likely to want to help you again!

I wanted to thank two local business people in a special way. So I had gourmet gift baskets sent to them. They both said that in all the years they had been in business, no one had ever bothered to thank them with a gift or do anything special for them. They were surprised and delighted.

One of the most valuable ways to maintain a positive attitude, have patience and stay fired up, as you pursue your dream, is to express gratitude for all the blessings in your life. You'll feel good too, because *being thankful is one of the main keys to happiness!*

Be optimistic. Look at challenging situations as opportunities to grow to the next level. Appreciate what you have but focus, with a positive attitude, on where you want to be, instead of the often momentary challenges at hand. Decide to be a happy, joyful person who attracts others like you! No one wants to be around a whiner.

And, remember, as Eddie Rickenbacker (former top ranking American fighter pilot and president of Eastern Airlines) once said, *"Think positively and masterfully, with confidence and faith, and life becomes more secure, more fraught with action, riches, in achievement and experience."*

Now Take These *Are You Fired Up?* Action Steps

- ♦ Read positive books to develop and maintain a winning attitude.
- ♦ Review your most recent challenge and look at it in a new way. Picture it as a successful learning and growing experience. Notice how you have benefited from it.
- ♦ When you find yourself talking to yourself negatively, say "Deflect" or "Cancel That."

Chapter 16

Using Affirmations to Build Your Dream

Add More Fuel To The Fire

"If one advances confidently in the direction of his dreams, and endeavors to live the life which he has imagined, he will meet with a success unexpected in common hours. "
Henry David Thoreau

Let Go of Negative Thinking

You probably have already seen the value of uncovering and replacing myths that you might have let stop you in the past. Perhaps you still have negative beliefs to let go of. One of the best ways to eliminate these is through the use of affirmations.

Are You Fired Up! **Principle #25—***Use Affirmations Daily*

Made popular over the last 20 years, affirmations are positive present tense statements that people say to themselves daily to help bring about change and increase self-esteem. Remember how the research says people have 40,000 to 50,000 thoughts a day and that 75-85 percent of them are negative? Change your internal self talk so it's all positive in support of your dreams. That's where affirmations help. Although experts' opinions vary about the exact number of days, it's generally believed that *any affirmation said consistently every day for 21-31 days* will change the programming of the subconscious. For particularly deep-seated myths, it may require a few months' worth of repeating affirmations. When you stick with the information, it will impact you. This may seem surprisingly simple, but affirmations work amazingly well. They can help you stay fired up and on track with your action plan.

Even Better than I Had Hoped

As the owner of an advertising and training company, I have discovered the value of affirmations when used in business. A few years ago, I learned that my office manager had the chance to go for her dream of living in Montreal, Canada. So, I encouraged her and began to search for a replacement. In addition to placing ads, I created a statement following all the guidelines given later in this chapter. It read "I am attracting the perfect employee to my business," and I kept repeating it each day in the shower. Within two weeks, a young man came to apply for the job.

While discussing his abilities, he casually mentioned that he also had experience as a graphic designer and showed me his portfolio, which was commendable. After interviewing several other applicants, I hired him.

This employee actually took on two jobs; that of office manager and graphic designer. His arrival also meant that I needed freelance designers less and less, which saved the company money. Indeed, the perfect employee had shown up—in ways I had never dreamed of. Hiring him got me fired up once more about the power of affirmations!

Letting Go of the Old and Affirming the New

In addition to that story, I have also experienced a number of great successes with affirmations over a period of several years. As a result of a difficult childhood, I learned to deal with some serious challenges. Such situations were a central part of my life, and it was exhausting coping with it all. So I decided to do something about it.

In 1988 I started using affirmations and decided that all experiences, whether positive or negative, were things for me to grow through, not just go through. Today, my life is very different. I'm very fortunate; I have a wonderful husband, a successful business, great friends, a beautiful, comfortable home, and two frisky, playful cats. I have more peace of mind now than I've ever had. Issues still come up, but I find they are usually small and manageable. Whatever happens, I work through it, learn from it and move on. I am healthy and my stress level has dropped significantly.

Why Do Affirmations Work?

One of the reasons affirmations work so well is that they help you refocus your thinking. Many times, people tend to focus on the problem rather than the solution, which just creates more of the problem. *You get what you focus on.* Focused concentration is a key to peak performance.

Focus on What You Want and Go for It!

If you are short on cash, concentrate on financial freedom. Most people just look at their unpaid bills and feel frustrated. If you want more money in your life, develop affirmations which fit your style and meet your needs. There are books devoted to gaining financial freedom, some with terrific affirmations, like: "My financial wealth increases daily, as I pursue my dreams." Another one is: "My wealth is dramatically increasing in a wide variety of ways."

Earl Nightingale, co-founder of Nightingale-Conant, started the company with a book called *The Strangest Secret.* In essence, the secret is, "You become what you think about most." Think about your dream, your successes and your abilities. Focus on what you want, not on what you don't want.

Affirmations alone won't bring about significant change; you also need to take action. Former U.S. President Calvin Coolidge, put it into perspective when he said, "We cannot do everything at once, but we can do something at once." Sitting at home all day saying affirmations about being a leader in your business or profession won't make you successful.

You need to focus on your dream and do whatever it takes to make it happen. However, affirming your success is a dynamic tool that can *assist* you in the process. It will train your mind to see yourself as a leader, which will help you bring the idea into reality. Affirmations are a great way to reeducate your subconscious about your capacity to succeed and to stay fired up about your life.

Guidelines for Creating Effective Affirmations

Repeating a poorly phrased affirmation can actually do more harm than good. It's the old adage: "Be careful what you ask for, you just might get it." For example, if the affirmation is "I am finding a 'new car' for very little money," you may be given your family's old clunker, only to find out that the transmission is broken! A better choice would be to say "I am finding the best, perfectly working, affordable car for me." By being more specific, you enhance your chances of finding the car for you.

Effective Affirmations:

♦ *Are always phrased in the positive.* When you say, "Don't think about polka dotted giraffes," what immediately comes to mind? Polka dotted giraffes! Focus on what you want—not on what you wish to change. For example, say "I am slim, energetic and healthy," rather than "I am no longer fat." Eliminate any words that cause you to have a negative picture. If you include the negative idea in your affirmation, you are unintentionally reinforcing what you don't want. You can't focus on the opposite of an idea.

◆ *Are stated in the present tense* using "I am," and often coupled with action verbs ending in "ing." (e.g. "I am easily finding the ideal prospects and clients for my business.") If someone says they *will be* healthy, that's always in the future—it's not now. You want to start picturing and experiencing the victory today, *right now.*

Remember, you can only take action when you are "living in the present"; you can't change the past and you can't live in the future. If there's a quality you want in the future, you need to affirm it in the present—otherwise it will always be out there someday. For example, say "I am totally healthy," rather than "I will be healthy tomorrow." Tomorrow is always in the future and someday becomes a new word called never. Make it happen *now!*

◆ *Are only about you.* If people create affirmations about others, it doesn't work. A mother may say, for example, "My son is cleaning his room tonight." Her affirmation won't help because it's up to her son to take action. What she could say instead is, "I have a beautiful and orderly house," and ask her son for help. Her affirmation is only effective for the actions *she* takes, which, in this case, is requesting her son's cooperation.

◆ *Need to have a visual picture associated with them.* If you say, "I am fired up about my dream," make sure you have a picture in your head of what being fired up looks like. You might envision yourself as excited, listening to your favorite tape, dressed for success and living your dream life. Or you may sense you're feeling positive and on track, knowing you're fulfilling your true purpose and picturing yourself as confident.

Whatever your affirmation means to you, get a clear vision of it mentally, so you can recognize it when you've achieved it. This is especially important when your affirmation is about a state of mind or something abstract. If you're affirming being a leader in your business or profession, you may want to imagine yourself relaxing with other leaders you know at a resort. Imagine yourself doing something you love to do, like golf, swim or walk on the beach.

Whatever it is, make sure you can see it in detail. If you want a big, beautiful house, what's it like in your mind? Is it a colonial, a cape, a contemporary, a ranch, a log cabin or another style? Is it brand new, just a few years old, a lovely older home or something else? Look through architectural magazines or house plan books and get a crystal clear picture of what you want. Put the details in your affirmation.

♦ *Need to have positive emotional components,* such as "I am *easily* and *happily* attracting *ideal* new associates and clients." Adding strong, positive emotion makes the affirmation seem more real to your subconscious. The best affirmations get you fired up about your goal.

A leader who'll be on stage at an upcoming business seminar might say, "I am excited and sharing my story with love, humility, and gratitude," to get fired up for the event. I personally like to add "easily" into affirmations because I want it to happen gracefully. So many people make life more difficult than it has to be— why not make it as easy as possible?

♦ *Need to be short enough to remember,* since you need to say them often. More than about 10-15 words is usually too much for the mind to hold. Try yours out for a day or two. If you find yourself forgetting the affirmation, you may want to reword it so it's catchy and memorable—like a slogan or jingle.

♦ *Need to be said every day,* at least once or twice a day, until something positive happens. Some affirmations may take several months or even years to achieve, while others may take effect in just a few weeks. It often depends on your answers to these three questions. 1) How deeply ingrained was your negative belief which the affirmation is replacing? 2) Have you let go of the negative belief? 3) Are you stretching towards a huge goal? Be aware that your affirmations may take more time to take effect than you believe they will, due to those variables. You need to keep moving towards your dream and be as patient as you can, until you achieve it. Affirmations work only when you *act* on them. As Thomas Henry Huxley once said, "The great end in life is not knowledge but action."

Record Your Affirmations

Here's a direct and effective method to help you ingrain your affirmations on your conscious and subconscious mind. Record them into a tape recorder. Talk to yourself enthusiastically. You could put your favorite instrumental music on in the background. Say your affirmation is "I am healthy and wealthy." Record it with passion.

Then do the same with the affirmation in second and third person i.e., "You, (your name), are healthy and wealthy" and "(Your name) is healthy and wealthy." Do this with all your affirmations. Play your tape in your bathroom or on your way to work. Start your day in a positive way. This can quickly help you to start replacing your old programming.

If you prefer not to tape record your affirmations—that's fine. Just be sure to say them every day for 21-31 consecutive days. If you miss a day, start over. Whether you record them or not, post them (which you may want to decorate with color or stickers) in a place where you'll see them daily.

Affirmations for Your Dream

Now, to use this new information to achieve your dream. Look at the next page, where the Dream Affirmations section appears. There's space for five affirmations. Take a few minutes now and think about the affirmations you could create to support your dream. These need to be statements that will assist you in achieving your goals. You are by no means limited to only five—just use five as a starting point.

For someone who is building their business or profession, one affirmation might read, "I am easily meeting and building relationships with the right people." Some other appropriate affirmations may be:

- ♦ "I have a clear and powerful vision for my business."
- ♦ "I do whatever it takes to achieve my dreams."
- ♦ "I am expanding my contact list daily."
- ♦ "I am building a strong team of leaders."
- ♦ "I have a strong client base."

They are short, emotional and present tense, providing a visual picture for them. Using these examples, you are now ready to create affirmations for yourself. Dedicate some time and energy to writing affirmations which will support *your* vision. Remember the guidelines, and have fun with this.

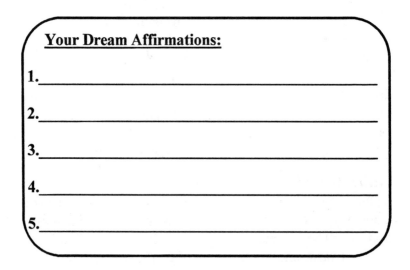

Your Dream Affirmations:

1. _____

2. _____

3. _____

4. _____

5. _____

The act of creating and writing down your affirmations sends a powerful message to your subconscious—that this is something you really want. You're starting to invest energy into making it happen. Affirmations help you move on from negative thinking patterns and adopt new thoughts and belief systems about yourself. You're taking control, rather than allowing the negative thoughts to affect you. You decide how you think and feel about yourself—you're in charge.

When you're developing affirmations for your dream, you're letting your subconscious know—*you are in charge of your dream.* Your dream is meaningful and worth whatever effort it takes to make it come true. You'll be amazed how the energy in your life relates to your vision, once you commit it to writing. You'll get fired up and make your dream come true.

Now Take These *Are You Fired Up?* Action Steps

♦ If you have not already done so, create affirmations for your dream. Say them 21-31 days in a row and act on them.

♦ To get even more value from your affirmations, record them on tape as described earlier in this chapter.

Chapter 17

Affirmations In Action

Showering Sparks On The Tinder

*"The key to staying fired up about your dream is
to keep taking action."*

Are You Fired Up? Principle #26—Use Action Options to Get Fired Up

The key to creating and using *effective* affirmations is very simple: *choice*. When you use action options to *choose* how you want to put your affirmations into action, you put yourself "in the driver's seat" which gets you fired up.

Sometimes when a person is trying to help someone resolve a situation, they tell them exactly what to do, giving them no choice. The problem is, *this can be felt as a form of control or manipulation*—even if it's unintentional. With at least three different options on how to take action, everyone is free to decide for themselves what works best for them. This is essential, because so many people have rigidly locked themselves into only one way of doing things.

Certain family structures have systems in place that force children to do things in only one way—the "right way." And while it may have been effective when we were children to follow those standards, it can be severely limiting and frustrating to use them as adults going for our dreams. In order to shift gears, and expand our horizons out of our comfort zones and grow, we all need to be flexible. Through options, we give ourselves permission and freedom to take appropriate action, while stimulating original thinking and creative solutions. *Choice liberates; singularity limits.*

Creating Your Own Action Options

Now refer to the Dream Affirmations list you completed in the last chapter. Take each of your affirmations and come up with at least three different action options to support each affirmation. Hint—*Look at your mind map and you will find many of the action options there.*

You are not committing to these actions at this point unless you want to. You are simply developing some choices of how you can make your dream happen and stay fired up. That means you can stretch and think big; the sky is the limit, and fires burn best when there's lots of fuel.

Do You Need More Money to Make Your Dream Come True?

It is often necessary to develop another source of income to live your dream fully. If you want to teach a large number of people, perhaps around the world, about something dear to your heart, and believe it's truly your mission, you are probably going to need lots of money to do it. There might be grants available; but it's more likely you'll have to earn the money yourself before you can fully live your dream. There's absolutely nothing wrong with that; it's a very smart and practical way to make things happen.

In college, I worked as a telemarketer for a roofing and siding company. When I was a teacher, I waitressed and worked in department stores. Today, there are many home-based businesses you can do, without affecting your job.

Bill wanted to spend more time with his family and own a car dealership. He started a home-based business while flying for the Airforce, and retired early. The income from his business enabled him to buy a beautiful horse farm as well as the dealership. He built his business and made his dreams come true. Today he is sought after as a speaker and trainer for business organizations around the world.

Remember—*the key to staying fired up about your dream is taking action.* So, let's get moving right now and stoke up your fire.

Now Take These *Are You Fired Up?* Action Steps

- ♦ If you have not already done so, develop three action options for each affirmation of your dream.
- ♦ Consider asking your leader or mentor for other ideas, so you have a long list of options.
- ♦ Schedule action items into your planner.

Chapter 18

Persistence and Achievement

The Tinder Begins To Glow

"Nothing in the world can take the place of persistence. Talent will not; nothing is more common than unsuccessful men with talent. Genius will not; Unrewarded genius is almost a proverb. Education alone will not; the world is full of educated derelicts. Persistence and determination alone are omnipotent."
Calvin Coolidge

Are You Fired Up? **Principle #27—*Finish What You Start***

This process has five basic phases: 1) Learn about or get an idea. 2) Understand and accept it. 3) Commit to it. 4) Take action on it. 5) Persist until you achieve the result.

The *first phase* is usually where you feel the initial excitement and start to get fired up about the possibilities of making your dream come true. You'll most likely share your enthusiasm with others.

This is also like the beginning part of a romantic relationship. It's that first phase of contact when everything the other person does is "perfect," and you're constantly thinking about them. Some people like the aspect of infatuation so much that they don't stay in relationships long enough for them to deepen into mature love and become more fulfilling. They are stuck in the first phase and then cheat themselves, believing this phase is the best part.

The *second phase* is when you understand and accept the idea, and take possession of it. This is where you actually sign-up for something or get involved. Ideally, this is followed by making a commitment, the *third phase*. Taking action on it is the *fourth phase*. Doing whatever it takes to achieve the results, the *fifth phase*, is necessary to make your dream come true. You need to persist.

Many people fail to commit to making it happen for themselves and their family. They take some action, but if they run into an obstacle they give up. They do something "halfway" but they don't fully commit. What is unfortunate about this besides, of course, their dreams not coming true, is that there is a special feeling of exhilaration that you experience every time you persist and achieve something. You feel good about yourself and it gets you fired up to accomplish your next dream. People who stay stuck at the understanding and accepting level never benefit from that. The great news is that we can change our thinking and behavior and get unstuck.

Finishing Is Essential—*Take Action Until You Succeed!*

Unfinished dreams and goals drain large amounts of energy. How does this happen? It can show up in dozens of ways, like half-read books and half-listened to tapes. It ranges from closets overflowing with clothes you haven't worn in years, to the classic "to do" lists that never get everything crossed off.

"What's wrong with that?" you may ask. The problem is that unfinished goals and dreams are a form of self-sabotage which can destroy your self-esteem. Every day, every one of us makes commitments or agreements to do things. Saying you'll be at work on time is an agreement. Setting up lunch with a friend or acquaintance at a certain time and place is an agreement. Saying you'll take out the garbage tonight is an agreement.

Every time you say to yourself or someone else that you will do things, you are making agreements. Some people call them commitments or promises. Most people are pretty good at keeping agreements with others. If they say they will meet someone at two o'clock, they do it. People who don't keep agreements don't have many friends, because they aren't reliable. You probably know people like this and maybe have even let them disappoint you. Remember, *broken agreements destroy relationships.*

What about agreements with yourself? This is where most of us need to focus our awareness and make some changes. Here's an example:

John goes to bed to take a short nap after supper, and realizes he hasn't phoned any prospects all week. So he sets his alarm clock for 7 p.m. and tells himself that he'll go to the phone and make calls for an hour.

When the alarm rings at 7, he flips on the TV. What has just happened? He let himself down. He has broken his agreement with himself and he feels miserable. If he does this enough times, he no longer believes his own word. His self-esteem slowly diminishes and he may feel tired and anxious. How can he overcome this?

Everything unfinished is a broken agreement and, as long as something is still hanging out there not completed, it saps a little bit of energy. Pile up enough unfinished business and you have a frustrated person who feels like a failure. That's what John may be experiencing, even if he won't admit it. Persistent committed action is rewarded and lack of commitment and inaction leads to stagnancy and failure.

Unfinished business is often linked to procrastination. People who procrastinate may do so for different reasons; from fear of failure to fear of success. Some people are comfortable with chaos and some feel so overwhelmed that they don't know where to begin. Some believe they work better under pressure, but let it build until it's super stressful. These are just a few of the ways people can limit their capacity to achieve.

How Can You Prevent Unfinished Business?

One way to do this is to use a time management system as described in Chapter 13. *Write every agreement down* in your planner, including agreements with yourself. Always keep your planner with you and refer to it several times a day. Put a check mark beside each agreement as it is successfully accomplished and feel your confidence growing.

Another technique is to say "no." Think carefully before agreeing to do anything. Determine whether you actually want to do it and can do it, considering your priorities. If you are unsure, don't commit to it.

For example, say your child is on the school soccer team and you've been asked to coach. For one thing, you may not want to do it. Secondly, even if you found the idea appealing, it would require a lot of evening and weekend hours. This may cut into the time you need to get ahead in your business or profession.

Therefore, you could reply, "I appreciate the confidence you have in me, but I already have a very busy schedule with a lot of commitments. No, I'm not the person to do it. Have you asked George or Harry?"

A third technique, as discussed earlier, is to *renegotiate the agreement.* Rather than breaking agreements, be clear that you are renegotiating.

You're making a mutually acceptable change. This enables you to maintain your integrity and self-esteem, and it creates trust and respect with your friends, loved ones, and others with whom you associate.

Clean Up Your Home Environment—*Dejunk*

Another powerful way to eliminate unfinished business and get your energy fired up is to— *look at how you live and physically take action.* To resolve the unfinished status of half-read books, develop a plan to complete them. Recycle papers, bottles, jars and cans. Clean out your closets and make room for new clothes. Take the old clothes you and your family no longer wear to a friend in need, to the Red Cross, the Volunteers of America, the Salvation Army, a church, a shelter for the homeless, or another charity in the country where you live. Throw out any old cans of food or half-eaten boxes of stale crackers.

Clean up your living environment and eliminate any clutter. Walk around your home and see which areas always catch your eye because they're messy. Most people have at least a couple of areas that need work. Resolve to take action, one step at a time, and organize them. Find a way to eliminate all the things you aren't using and either sell them or give them away to a charity, or to someone else who can use them. In other words—*dejunk!*

Some nonprofit organizations, like Volunteers of America, will even come to your home and pick up all your useable items that you are getting rid of. This is a powerful and positive exercise. One woman cleaned out all of her closets. The next week, as a surprise, her husband gave her three new dresses. She had made room for the new clothes by getting rid of the old ones!

Finish what you start. Do what you said you would do, when you have completed the task, you've kept the agreement. With finishing comes a release of confident energy, a sense that you are a successful, powerfully focused person who gets things done. That energy and attitude can help you go a long way towards achieving your dreams and being fired up. Persist until you achieve your goal!

Agreements About Your Dream

Now let's return to your dream, the one you have been working with throughout the book. Go to your list of Affirmations and Actions Options from Chapter 17 and your Action Worksheet. You have listed at least 15 different actions you could take to move on your dream. Now cover stage three—the commitment phase—where you choose which agreements you need to take action on and you decide when.   Write down the specific action option you are choosing to do, a target date and the date when the action was actually completed.

For example, a man wanted to create significant sums of money for a wildlife project. One of his affirmations was about gaining financial freedom through his own business. He had three action options on how to do that. So he chose which ones he wanted to do and made a time commitment. He accomplished the first action step by the date he set and the second one he completed earlier. His next step was to list all the other action steps he wanted to take with target dates.

Now it's time for you to take more action on your dream. Make your action steps *small, clear and realistic*. For example, it's wiser to have an action step like: "Go to the auto show and meet five new positive people," rather than just "meet some people." The more specifically and clearly the step is stated, the more likely you will accomplish it.

Review your action options, get out your planner, and set some optimistic goals. For example, schedule ten appointments for your business or profession in a given week. That way, if you get cancellations or "no shows," you can still meet your goal of five activities that week. Before you set your goal, be sure to think of how you will reward yourself. It's important not to work just for work's sake. Give yourself incentive to keep going by knowing ahead of time how you're going to celebrate your accomplishment. For example, after you've met your goals every week for a month, you could take your family out for a nice dinner.

And finally, after you have made your list of action steps with target dates, see yourself as successful. Remember that many professional athletes in basketball, tennis, golf and other sports first visualize their success; they see themselves winning and they often do. They get themselves fired up. Every play, swing, and movement is seen perfectly and clearly. When they are actually playing the sport, they are much more likely to do so with excellence.

Some of them, like Tara Cross Battle, 1996 Olympic member of the U.S. Women's Volleyball team, use music to inspire and motivate themselves. Tara listens to gospel music before games. "It gets me fired up and ready to go," she explains.

Take a few minutes now and put on some inspiring music. See yourself fired up and successfully taking action on each one of these steps by the target date. Allow yourself to experience it fully. Feel all the positive emotions and energy; hear the cooperative comments from others you ask for help. *Picture ease and success every step of the way.* When you can see yourself succeeding, you're halfway there. That's great! You can do it!

Now Take These *Are You Fired Up?* Action Steps

- ♦ If you have not already done so, do the finishing activity in this chapter.
- ♦ If you have not done so, take out your Action Plan and commit to taking action. Schedule your action steps into your time management system.
- ♦ Play music that gets you fired up. Play it whenever you want to think about or are working on your dream.
- ♦ Persist until you achieve your dream.

Chapter 19

Paint Your Picture of Success

Stoking the Fire

*"The most important thing in your life is to live your life
for something more than your life."*
William James

A New Way to Picture Your Dreams

Now you're ready to take your dream one step further, by
using your vision to create a powerful tool—a dream
collage—to help you succeed.

Are You Fired Up? **Principle #28—***Create a Dream
Collage*

A dream collage, or treasure map as some call it, is a
visual representation of your completed successful dream. It
is a terrific way to stay fired up about it. It starts with colored
poster board or foamcore, perhaps covered with your favorite
colored wrapping paper. You paste up pictures and words
that represent your fully achieved dream on this board.

You can create these images, cut them from magazines
and newspapers, or use photographs you have taken. A
combination of all these things would be great, too. One of
the most important elements of your dream collage is that

your picture is on it—put yourself in the dream to make it seem more real and personal.

Are You Fired Up? **Principle #29—*Let the Little Child Inside Your Heart Come Out and Play***

Have you ever been to an amusement park and watched the adults? You'll notice many adults there without children; yet they're laughing and playing anyway. One of the reasons Disney World is so successful is that adults get to be kids there, too.

Inside each of our hearts is a spontaneous, happy child. Some people are good at inviting this fun loving child to come out and play; while others keep them locked away. It's essential that you invite the child inside your heart to participate in your dream. That child is very creative, knows no boundaries, and thinks only in terms of possibilities. You can benefit by connecting with and accessing these gifts. This is especially true when you're creating your dream collage.

Lisa wanted to build her business and create a happy married life. Within a year of creating her dream collage, she was happily married to her new husband, and sharing her successful business with him. Lisa has experienced more joy than ever before, and continues to grow and improve her life. She actually has a different collage for every area of her life—finances, health, family, business and such. She has placed the collages in key places around her house, so almost everywhere she looks there's a collage.

Making My Dreams Come True with a Collage

I have personally had tremendous results with dream collages. In 1989 I created a collage, mainly focusing on my personal life. I wasn't married yet, and I wanted to find a great husband. So I picked out key words to get me fired up like "The Best Man Ever." I cut out a picture of a wedding dress I liked, along with pictures of places I wanted to visit with my new husband. In the upper left hand corner, I put a picture of myself with words from a magazine that said "Her Brilliant Career," "High Profile Creativity" and "Women to Watch in the 1990's." These phrases kept the flame alive inside of me and inspired me to achieve. There were also photos of sailboats, since that's my favorite hobby, plus other meaningful words and pictures. Here's an example of a dream collage:

To help you build your dream, create your own dream collage. Here's some ideas of what you could do. First, put a picture of yourself and your spouse in the center.

Include the level, position, or title you want to achieve in your business or profession under your photo. If you enjoy travelling, get some brochures with pictures of your favorite places. Put the name of the location with the photo. Cut pictures out of magazines to represent sports you like such as golfing, hot air ballooning, sailing, and flying. If you want a new boat, airplane or something else, include them.

Cut out or take pictures of your dream home, jewelry, car(s), motorcoach or anything else you want. Include intangible dreams like "healthy and wealthy," "debt-free," "financially free," or "time with your family." Do what suits you and have fun with it.

After your collage is completed, take a photo of it. Get some color enlargements to put up around your house and some reductions that fit your wallet. See your dreams in front of you as often as possible. This will help keep you motivated by reminding you what you're striving for.

With the exception of the trip to Australia, which we're going to take at a later date, *everything on my collage has come true!* In 1991 I married "The Best Man Ever" in a dress similar to the one on the collage which I designed and had custom made. We went to the Caribbean for our honeymoon and have since chartered large sailboats there. I exercise and take care of myself.

The most surprising thing about the collage was something I never would have predicted. That little upper left-hand corner for and about my career, "High Profile Creativity," came true in incredible ways. In 1991 I received a national award from the Small Business Administration for my work in helping to create a non-profit organization to help women start and stay in business. That award resulted in my flying to Washington DC., and going to a ceremony in the Rose Garden at the White House with then President Bush. Seven of us were honored at a Congressional luncheon with over 700 people. This led to exposure in national magazines.

Based on my personal experience, dream collages are powerful and effective. My husband, Spencer, and I now have a couple's dream collage for our life together. It covers every aspect from romance and travel, to our spiritual life and finances. It's about five feet long and resides in our bedroom. We look at it regularly for inspiration and to keep on track.

Now It's Your Turn

Schedule an entire morning, afternoon or evening for this activity, because it can make a big difference in your ability to focus on your dream. It's fun, engrossing and well worth the time you invest. You'll be amazed at how real your dreams become and how fired up you get looking at them. Here's what you need to get started:

♦ A large piece of poster board or foamcore.
♦ Tape or glue.
♦ Magazines with the topics and themes that reflect your dream.
♦ Construction paper and markers to make words and pictures.
♦ A photo of yourself.
♦ A pair of scissors.
♦ Your imagination.

Where Do You Get Your Ideas?

Focus on your dream description and action plan for now, for one year, for three years and for five years from now. Imagine you are painting a picture of your success that fully portrays all you want to create and live as your dream. Look for pictures and words in magazines and cut out everything that appeals to you. You can also use photographs. Take your time and make sure what you want is completely represented. If you need additional money for your dream, draw a pot of gold or show dollar signs. You might want to consider putting the word "easy" on your collage to help you believe you can achieve your dream with ease. Definitely *include a picture of yourself* in the collage—this is essential to your ability to see yourself as successful.

Once you have all the pieces of your collage, including all the words, photos and graphics you want, including the picture of yourself, review them to be sure each item on the board clearly communicates what you want. *Be specific.*

Here's a great idea. Write a fake check to yourself for a large sum of money, say $1,000,000, and put it on your

Here's a great idea. Write a fake check to yourself for a large sum of money, say $1,000,000, and put it on your collage. The more you see it, the more familiar and comfortable you become with the idea of having $1,000,000!

Make your collage colorful, so your dreams come "alive" when you look at it. Test each picture emotionally—does it get you fired up or not? If not, leave it off your dream collage. A good way to find out is if you get "goosebumps" or some other positive reaction. This indicates the picture has meaning and value for you.

Once you're happy with all the pieces of the collage, lay them out on the board, which may be in color or covered in your favorite glittery wrapping paper. Play with the layout and move things around until everything looks just right, and then tape or glue them down.

Once the glue has dried, put your collage where you will see it every day. A good location is the refrigerator door. Look at it daily—*notice how you're doing and give yourself credit for your successes.* Let it get you fired up and help you move closer and closer towards achieving your dreams; just like it did for Sally.

A Dream Come True

Sally Garrett's lifelong dream was to go to Africa to study wildlife. As a student at Antioch College in New England, she began to find ways to make her dream come true.

First, she created a large dream collage which she hung on her bulletin board. It was covered with pictures of Africa, a *National Geographic* map, and a photograph from a camera catalog where the lens focused on a wild heron—with a notepad and pencil nearby. It expressed completely what she wanted to be doing—studying wildlife. Sally studied her dream collage daily; she visualized herself living her dream, and took consistent action. In the fall of 1991 she set out to make her dream come true. At Antioch, she met with a

Africa. That led her to connect with Professor Bill Barklow, who had just received a study grant for Tanzania.

Between October 1991 and June 1992, Sally scrambled to create the resources to go to Africa; she depleted her savings and had to rush through her final classwork so she could make the trip. She booked three different sets of flight reservations for Tanzania, not knowing when the expedition would be leaving or if she would be part of it. Finally, she got word that the departure date was in June and she would be conducting research on hippopotamus communication.

Alone and completely fired up, this courageous woman traveled across the ocean to Tanzania, "the most foreign place" she had ever experienced. Nearly missing her connection with the safari, she joined the expedition and headed for the bush. There she spent her days observing two groups of hippos and their interactions with each other. She fondly remembers that first night happily thinking, "I am living my dream. This is wonderful and it's real." Sally had never felt more confident or fulfilled in her life.

Many adventures challenged her courage and thinking abilities during her time in Africa. For example, she got stranded overnight on a local bus, and was criticized by negative-thinking people because she was traveling alone. But she triumphed over the difficulties and ended up spending four exciting months in Tanzania, Kenya, and Zimbabwe.

The fact that she had succeeded in making her dream come true gave her a reserve of courage which she needed when she went home. Shortly after her return, she came face to face with some serious family difficulties. But the act of having achieved her dream, of having her dream collage come true so perfectly, served to spur her on and keep her going, no matter what challenges she faced. As she says now, "Once you know you have made your dream come true, you know you can do it again. It's just a question of

choosing what dream to work on. I can do anything now."
Sally's courage and success have helped to inspire her to
keep going as well as fired up others.

Now you have a powerful and exciting dream collage to
work from. Show it only to positive thinking people who
will encourage you, believe in you and appreciate your
dream. Other than that, keep it to yourself. Congratulations
on your work! You have made a terrific tool for helping you
realize your dreams.

Now Take These *Are You Fired Up?* Action Steps

♦ If you have not done so already, create your own dream
collage.

♦ Once your completed collage has dried, put it where
you'll see it every day, like the refrigerator door. Focus
on it every day, notice how you're doing and give
yourself credit for your successes. Let it get you fired
up and move you closer and closer towards achieving
your dream.

Chapter 20

Avoid Dream-Delaying Hooks

Keep Smoldering Embers Alive

"Whether you think you can or think you can't,
you're right."
Henry Ford

Are You Fired Up? **Principle #30—***Avoid the Hooks***

Do you remember the old vaudeville acts where a performer would be all fired up singing or dancing, and a giant hook would come out and pull the person offstage in mid-act? Or perhaps you've seen the comedy "The Gong Show," where judges would gong the entertainer if they didn't like him. That entertainer's dream of performing would be over, at least for that show.

That's what is meant by *hooks to avoid.* They're the real-life hooks that'll be obstacles if you allow them to be. They can only douse the flames of your enthusiasm and discourage you from going further on your dream, if you let them. Knowing about these hooks, ahead of time, can help you to be on the alert so you can prevent them from stopping you.

While people's dreams vary, many want to directly touch others' lives in a positive way. They want to have personal contact with those who benefit from what they have to offer. They can't afford to let dream-delaying hooks get in the way.

Reaching Out to Relatives

Sam and Virginia had been married for ten years and had two children. One day they looked at each other and said, "Is this all there is?" We just go home to work and work to home, over and over again. And, we never seem to get anywhere. It's like being on a treadmill. When are we going to get out of this boring routine and live our dreams?"

Later that week they were all visiting Sam's brother Ed and his wife Gloria who live in the next town. At dinner, Virginia remembered their "Is this all there is?" conversation and shared it. Sam and Virginia had no idea that Ed and Gloria had their own independent business and could help them get out of their rut.

The following week, Ed called Sam and asked if he and Gloria were serious about wanting to move on. Sam said yes and they set-up a time to get together.

It was a gratifying experience to see how Sam and Virginia regained the hope they once had for a better life. Ed and Gloria felt like they were making a positive difference in Sam and Virginia's lives. The great bonus is, they became even closer as a family as they built their businesses together.

This example has people as a key component, on the giving and receiving ends. They need to help other people for their dream to be fully realized. For those who help others, it is especially vital to avoid dream delaying hooks.

Hook # 1—*Anticipated Outcomes*

If you let what others do or don't do affect your happiness, you're in for an emotional rollercoaster ride. The outcome of service can never be fully guaranteed or anticipated. If people who are helping others let their self-esteem be affected by how the helpee responds, there can be disappointments.

If, in the above example, Sam and Virginia had said no to Ed and Gloria, that probably means they weren't *really* looking for a change. Remember, a lot of people complain about their situation, but won't do anything about it! Ed and Gloria shouldn't take it personally. They need to keep going through the noes to get to the yesses.

The approach to take when you are working on a dream which involves others is to always maintain the philosophy of "for the greatest benefit of all concerned." That way, there are no hooks, and you can give your best without being attached to the outcome. This is sometimes referred to as "high commitment, low attachment." You work on your dream; you give it your full effort, but you aren't devastated if things don't turn out the way you hoped they would. You are fired up and focused on achieving your goals, but you're also open to what is best for everyone involved.

You need to maintain determination and persist until you make your dream come true. And at the same time, remain unattached to the final outcome. How do you do this?

The key is to have targeted results which are measurable and enable you to see that the work you do is helping others. Realize that if you touched even one person with your efforts—*your work has been worthwhile.* Make your daily success lists and acknowledge the "baby" steps and "microscopic" changes, along with your bigger achievements. Realize that even small achievements add up to significant improvements over time; they're part of the process.

Hook # 2—*Expecting a Specific Response*

Another hook is waiting for a particular response from those being helped. As I've journeyed through life, I found that *other people's behavior is about themselves—not us.* Up until I realized this, I had naively and egotistically thought that my actions were what caused other people to behave the way they did. Once I perceived how true this was—that other people behave a certain way because of what is going on in *their* lives—it gave me a great deal of freedom to just be myself and not be upset by the behavior of others.

The boss may *not* be yelling because he's unhappy with your job performance; he may have just had an argument with his wife and is venting his anger. The child in the cancer wing who won't smile at a volunteer's funny stories may be too sick from chemotherapy to notice anything else. The homeless person who received the coat someone donated may not say, "thank you" because of their shame about being homeless.

A prospective clients or associate may say no simply because of their situation. They're not rejecting you as a person. The point is, and it bears repeating—*other people's behavior is always about themselves.*   It's important to remember that when you are sharing or reaching out to others. Don't take on their emotional reactions as a personal affront. Stay focused on where you're going and feel good about what you are doing—*regardless of how others may react.*

Hook # 3—*Quitting Too Soon*

When you have a large or complex dream, it may take time and considerable effort to achieve it.   Building a big business, writing a book, and creating a brand new program for children, are all examples of long-term dreams.   What happens sometimes is that the dreamer quits too soon, often just short of achieving their dream.

Remember when we talked about finishing what you start, and how many people never do? They rob themselves of the significant satisfaction and burst of energy which results from completion.   Sometimes they quit because they are impatient, or because they are not seeing the results they want fast enough. Another reason they may quit is they allow the finite box of their imagination limit them. As Winston Churchill once said, *"Never, never, never, never give in...."*

Hook # 4—*Overlooking Small Victories Along the Way*

We all need to know we are making progress on our goals. We may be impatient with the process and want to see immediate results.   The culture in the U.S. is into instant gratification—buy now, pay later. (This may be true for the country you live in as well.)   Television teaches you that weight loss can be instant and permanent with this or that product.   Commercials show that the right breath mint can endear you to others.

The truth is, most dreams take time and require multiple steps before they come true.   Success is a journey, not a destination.   Keeping this in mind, as you keep doing whatever it takes, helps you to stay fired up.

Charting daily successes will keep you fired up and motivated, so that you know you're on your way. If, for example, a physical therapist felt like a failure because his patient with a broken leg wasn't able to walk normally in one day, he would be missing the big picture. Most dreams take time to come true; most require long-term consistent action to be realized. Recognizing the progress along the way is essential—it's a key piece of finishing what you start.

Now Take These *Are You Fired Up?* Action Steps

- ◆ Look over your dream descriptions. Notice if any of the hooks in this chapter apply to you, and take action to avoid them.
- ◆ Take two actions today toward your dream, and make it a daily habit.
- ◆ Acknowledge the successes you've had this week. Write them down and give yourself credit for having accomplished them.

Chapter 21

Keep Growing

Building the Fire Bigger

"The real secret of success is enthusiasm. Yes, more than enthusiasm, I would say excitement. I like to see people get excited. When they get excited, they make a success of their lives. You can do anything if you have enthusiasm. Enthusiasm is the sparkle in your eye, it is the swing in your gait, the grip of your hand, the irresistible surge of your will and your energy to execute your ideas."
Walter Chrysler

Be Positive

Staying fired up while pursuing your dream is an ongoing process that requires conscious awareness. Monitoring your progress is useful, but knowing what keeps your fire burning and energizes you is even more valuable.

All of us have had negative experiences. If you miss a good opportunity, get hurt physically or emotionally, or are criticized, you may tend to respond negatively.

The natural human reaction is to turn inward and lick your wounds However, there is a much more effective way of dealing with negativity. Shift into a positive attitude—*look for the lesson in the negative experience and grow from it.*

This story demonstrates the point. To most people, witnessing war-torn Bosnia would be negative. Seeing all the people suffering and the children who were orphaned would melt almost anyone's heart—like it did Gerry McClure's. She and her mother visited Bosnia in 1993 for two weeks, supplying badly needed medical supplies to a refugee center. Gerry was deeply affected by the children's pain. When she returned, her father's diagnosis of terminal cancer further shook her; she knew she needed to do something to make a difference.

Inspiration came to her in a dream and led to the birth of a new business specifically *designed to benefit children.* She started Heaven on Earth, Inc., a company which manufactures several different multiracial and non-denominational dolls meant to represent guardian angels. A minimum 10 percent of pretax profits are donated to worldwide charities.

Each "Angel Gram" doll's tag reads, *"This angel comes to you from above with the message of joy and God's love."* The dolls are available in black, white, Hispanic, and Asian; each one also has a cassette of the song, "Your Angel's Always There," an angel pendant for the child to wear, a *Little Book of Angels,* and a map showing where the donations from Heaven on Earth have gone around the world.

With six employees and revenues of over $1 million, the business has been able to donate monies and supplies to the Croatian Emergency Relief Fund, the Children's Welfare Institute in China, and International God-Parenthood to Bosnian Children, among others. Gerry's negative experience led to her realizing that she wanted to *share love and give a sense of hope to others.*

What's Negative and Positive for You?

As you work on your dream, identify which activities are negative and which are positive for you. This will help you be more aware and keep pointed in the direction you want to go. Spending more time in a positive state will enable you to think bigger, do more and create better results. It keeps your fire blazing.

Positive actions are those which help you feel better about yourself, stronger, more successful, and more competent. For some people, a positive action might be seeing an uplifting movie, getting a hug or going to a seminar. For others, it might mean doing something you have never done before, just for the fun of it.

These are in sharp contrast to negative activities—those actions which make you shut down, feel small, weak, tight, depressed, or incompetent. Watching violent TV shows or the negative news, spending time complaining about things or criticizing others; all these tend to put people in a negative state of mind.

Choose Positive Activities

Knowing what is positive and negative for you assists you in making conscious shifts in behavior and attitude. You'll purposely seek positive activities, especially if you're tired or depressed. In general, people who are the most effective in achieving their dreams and staying fired up regularly participate in positive, uplifting activities and avoid or transform negative behavior into something positive. They tend to be goodfinders.

Consciously choosing to attend a motivational seminar is an example of how this awareness works. If you choose to stay at home or watch TV, which often feeds into negative thinking, you're likely to feel even less motivated than when you turned it on. On the other hand, when you associate with positive people, you feel like you have accomplished something. Spending time with upbeat, supportive friends and role models benefits you more than visiting the office whiners. All of these are the kinds of choices you make daily.

Here is a way to help you determine what is positive or negative for you. A series of activities is listed with a blank next to each one. It's important to note that there are no right or wrong answers; there is only information. The same action may be positive to some, yet negative to others. It just depends on what you like to do.

Positive or Negative Activities—*An Exercise*
Put a P in the blank for Positive if it lifts you when you do it, and an N in the blank if this activity is Negative and brings you down.

_____ Exercising

_____ Being under pressure

_____ Rushing somewhere

_____ Meeting someone new

_____ Going sailing

_____ Napping

_____ Doing paperwork

_____ Going to work

_____ Being in nature

_____ Watching funny movies

_____ Honoring your spouse

_____ Taking a hot bath

_____ Swimming

_____ Traveling

_____ Smiling

_____ Reading the newspaper

_____ Grocery shopping

_____ Doing the laundry

_____ Starting a new project

_____ Eating

_____ Serving others

_____ Reaching a goal

_____ Cleaning out the closet

_____ Seeing friends

_____ Going to a seminar

_____ Dancing

_____ Jogging

_____ Paying bills

_____ Hugging

_____ Having a messy house

_____ Budgeting

_____ Staying indoors

_____ Playing with children

_____ Writing letters

_____ Being judged

_____ Singing

_____ Listening to music

_____ Arguing

_____ Reading

_____ Watching the news

_____ Cooking

_____ Painting/drawing

_____ Completing a project

_____ Playing basketball

_____ Crying

_____ Sharing successes

_____ Dreambuilding

_____ Playing with pets

Now that you've completed the list, you can learn more about yourself. Some people love to do the laundry because it's a completion, with clean clothes as a result. They focus on the prize. Others view it as a chore—they focus on the price. Some dread meeting new people, while others look forward to it with eager anticipation. They are excited about expanding their network of friends and acquaintances.

You may have also found that your answer would have been different had you imagined other specifics. For example, seeing certain friends might be positive; while seeing other "friends" might be a negative experience.

There are moments when paperwork can be really satisfying; and other times when it simply stacks up and you may feel overwhelmed. All that matters here is that you *learn what works for you.* Highlight all the P (Positive) activities in your favorite color and keep the list for future reference. Be sure to add other activities that are positive for you that aren't on the list. Depending on your priorities, it may not be the time to do some of these things. But you'll find that just thinking about them can get you fired up.

Any time you find yourself getting negative, learn from the experience and deliberately do or think about something positive. Better than that, plan your day around the kinds of experiences you would like to have; those that stir your sparks, set you on fire and move you closer to your dream. No matter what you do, though, *focus on the prize,* not the price.

For me, some of my most positive experiences have involved travel and exploration. I studied a little art and sculpture in prep school. (My mother had been an artist.) I was looking forward to seeing the work of Michelangelo when I visited Italy. But no one could have prepared me for my reaction to Michelangelo's David. This mammoth sculpture is in Florence, and I wasn't even sure where in the museum it was located. Flipping through my guidebook, I wandered from room to room until I entered the hall where David was showcased. I took one look and burst into tears. It was spectacular. I didn't expect to react like that—but I was moved by the incredible beauty of the statue. I remembered Michelangelo had said that he had simply cut away all the rock that wasn't a part of David!

Years later, I had a similar experience in Paris. The impressionist paintings of Renoir and Monet used to be housed in a quaint museum called Le Jeu du Pomme. When I climbed the stairs and came face to face with Monet's sailing paintings, again, I started crying. I don't know what came over me; I don't usually burst into tears. I was just deeply moved by the beauty and magnificence of what I was witnessing. These were positive activities for me and are treasured memories.

You may have had moments like these. When you choose your activities wisely, with the intention of staying open and positive, you are much more likely to be moving forward gracefully. Your dreams can then be attained much more easily. The fire can be stoked at every level, and the blaze can burn brighter and brighter.

Now Take These *Are You Fired Up?* Action Steps

♦ If you have not already done so, complete the positive and negative activity in this chapter.

♦ Schedule positive activities into your time/activity management system.

♦ Ask your leader or mentor, your spouse or a friend, to help you transform a negative experience into a positive one. Look for the lessons and change your thinking about the outcome.

Chapter 22

27 Tips For Staying Fired Up!

Keep the Fire Burning

*"Into each life comes a time to grow when dreams must
be spoken and wings must be tried... so reach for your dreams,
spread your new wings and fly."*
Florence Littauer

Are You Fired Up? **Principle #31—***Do What Winners Do to Stay Fired Up!*

You've read stories about famous athletes and heroes who kept going no matter what. They stayed fired up and achieved their dreams. Even those skilled in personal development have times when it's more difficult to stay motivated, and that's what this chapter is all about. It's chock full of tips which will help you get fired up and stay fired up. Use them regularly, especially if you get stuck. If one doesn't do it for you, try another until you get going again just keep moving and keep igniting the sparks of your fire.

Count Your Blessings

Before you review the tips, *consider your many blessings, write them down and be grateful for them.* No matter what your circumstances may be, there are positive aspects to your life, as the following story illustrates.

Becky Ferry is a teenage girl who knows all about what it takes to be a champion. She cares for Jersey cows on the family farm, many of which are blue ribbon winners. What is extraordinary is not that the cows are winners or even that Becky takes great pleasure in their victories. What is noteworthy is Becky's winning attitude after all the tragedy she has faced in her young life.

When she was nine years old, Becky's coat got caught on the spinning shaft of a machine that unloads corn from a wagon. Before anyone could stop the machine, she suffered multiple fractures of both her knees and legs. The only safe medical solution was amputation.

Incredibly, the first thing Becky asked when she came out of surgery was, "Will I be able to show cows again?" Her enthusiasm and fired up attitude have carried her a long way, through the grueling months of rehabilitation and physical therapy. She has been fitted with prosthetics, but finds them unwieldy for farm work. When working with her beloved cows, she prefers to wear her "stubbies"—short wide rubber platforms which give her stability and balance but not height.

In spite of her physical disability, she maintains a "B" average at school and works with the cows ten hours a day. She recently learned to swim again, and looks forward to a future filled with promise, including raising heifers. Her favorite cow, Sunny, a honey colored Jersey, earned the coveted Farmer's Museum Dairy Cup. Becky accepted the award with joy, as she was truly grateful and fired up. That's her fundamental outlook on life and it keeps her going every day. We could all learn a great deal from Becky's attitude.

Remember These Two Examples

Wilma Rudolph, the first woman runner to win three gold medals at a single Olympic event, overcame severe physical disabilities to become an athlete. At four, she was struck with double pneumonia and scarlet fever, losing the use of her left leg. Her family had a fired up attitude, though, and began massaging her leg four times a day. By age 11 she was able to run normally, and by high school she was an outstanding athlete. As a black Southern woman in the U.S., her challenges were many. But she beat them all to triumph at the Olympics and was named to the Women's Sports Hall of Fame.

Ski instructor Pete Seibert was called crazy when he told others about his dream. From age 12 on, he had the dream of building a top-level ski resort in Colorado. Without money, but with lots of vision and focus, he enrolled others in his dream. He got them fired up and went on to create and develop one of the most famous resorts in the U.S.—Vail, Colorado.

The 27 Tips for Staying Fired Up!

There are detailed explanations of each tip on the next several pages. They are tried and true ways to stay fired up. Find the ones that appeal to you the most, while not interfering with your priorities. Perhaps you will even discover some new ones.

Do whatever it takes to keep yourself fired up! Be a good example for others and keep moving and growing towards your dream.

Get fired up, stay fired up, and live your dream.

1. Identify What You Truly Want in Your Life

Periodically, update your dream list for life. Often, we change faster than we realize, and what was once important to us no longer is. College majors are good examples. Many students pick a major as a freshman, and choose another by their junior year. It's not unusual for someone to go all the way through school and find that their major is not what they want to do after all. The same may well be true in your life, and you may be ready for a change now. Your career may be something totally new a decade from now, and your life's work may shift substantially.

Remember the technique where you listed the circumstances in your life which you don't want? (You can review it in Chapter 3.) Every once in a while, make a new list to see where you are. It will help keep you clear about what you truly value and gets you fired up about life.

2. Dreambuild Regularly

Dreambuild as often as you can. It makes your dream seem more reachable. Go drive your dream car. Tour houses you'd like to live in. Go to car shows, boat shows, air shows, hobby shows, and the like. Take pictures of your dream and have someone else snap photos of you with the dream. Stay in touch with your dream and meet other dreamers.

Some of the greatest relationships you'll ever build can begin at those places, with people who have something in common with you. This makes it easier for you to "build the bridge" to a new relationship. Do this regularly to keep yourself fired up about where you're going. These activities are fun, free or inexpensive, don't take much time, and can be a key way for you to expand the number of people you know—a prime ingredient for any success.

3. Keep Agreements With Yourself and Others

Agreements are described throughout this book. Remember, every commitment you make to yourself and others is an agreement. Every time you break an agreement, you are sabotaging yourself and your self-esteem. If you find your life just isn't working—*take a look at your agreements.* Fulfill them or renegotiate them. Write them down. And, when you make an agreement, keep it.

4. Update Your Dream Collage and Regularly Picture Your Dream as Completed

Your dream collage is a dynamic tool for actually seeing your dream come to life. To many people, seeing is believing. Look at your collage daily to help you believe through seeing. Update it regularly with current pictures, words and symbols as you find your dreams coming true. Either change your dream collage or replace it as needed.

Clearly picture your dream fulfilled. Every time you do, it's likely you will experience something special and some new aspect of your dream will appear. The more clearly you envision your dream—*the sooner you're likely to be living it.*

5. Maintain a Daily Success List

I've suggested this several times throughout the book because it really helps you to teach yourself that you are successful. Through these lists, you'll learn to recognize how much you really do accomplish. Every time I feel like I'm not getting anywhere on my dream, I remember to do my daily success list. In a short period of time, my whole attitude shifts and I am fired up again about what I have done and what I am going to do. You can get fired up too.

6. Create a "Feel Good Folder"

In Chapter 13, I mentioned a miniature Feel Good Folder you could put in a zipper-type section in the back of your planner. Since the Feel Good Folder is such a great tool to help you overcome disappointments and stay fired up it's worth the effort to create one to keep at home.

You could use a folder, box or envelope—brightly colored or covered with attractive wrapping paper, if you want. Put things in it that you feel good about every time you see them. These can be things such as thank you notes, special letters, cards, cartoons, and victory symbols like awards, certificates, trophies and other items. Look for anything which inspires you or gets you fired up.

Include photos of loved ones, daily success lists, some of the forms you've completed in this book, pictures of vacation spots you'd like to visit, and any cars that really touch your heart. It's especially important to include an inventory of your strengths (positive traits) which will help you make your dreams come true.

Take a few minutes now to write down your positive attributes. A good rule of thumb is to list at least 25 qualities that will support you in winning. Number your paper from 1-25 and let the ideas pop into your head. Be kind to yourself and acknowledge the great person you are. Once you've finished, read over the list and appreciate yourself. Then put it in your Feel Good Folder.

7. Keep a "Reward/Pamper Yourself Jar" and Use it After You Have Taken Consistent Action on Your Dream for a Month

For example, say you gave a business presentation five times a week, or held ten classes, or made ten calls to prospects every day. After you've done great work on your dream, reward yourself. That's so the dreamer inside your heart gets involved in the process and you stay motivated.

Some people enjoy the reward process so much that they use a "Reward/Pamper Yourself Jar." This is a jar or bottle which you fill with various pieces of colored paper with rewards written on them. They might say "Get a therapeutic massage," "Have dinner with your best friend," "Take a bubble bath," "Entertain friends," or "Go dancing." Whatever you consider to be a reward, that's what you write down. Fill the jar with all these goodies and pull one every time you have taken consistent action on your dream for a month. It will get you fired up to do more and go for it again next month. After a while, you'll have such momentum with your success inducing habits, you may not need the reward system anymore! You'll be better at blending your fun with your business or profession.

8. Update Your Action Plan or Make a New One

The fired up Action Plan for Dreambuilding appears throughout the book. It's a valuable tool to help you focus on any goal or dream. Use it any time you have a new dream that you want to be fired up about to make it happen. It will ignite you into action.

9. Create an "Expanding Your Self-Definition" List

As you move on your dream, you will need to overcome obstacles and break through old fears. Be sure to record these experiences as you track your successes. Pay attention to them. They are important landmarks as you grow and change. They will forever change your self-perception. Refer to them often as examples of how you've grown. As Oliver Wendell Holmes once said, *"The mind, once expanded to the dimensions of a larger idea, never returns to its original size."*

10. Be of Service to Someone Else

One of the most powerful ways to shift your state to positive from negative is to serve someone else. It helps to focus on others. The key to service is that it comes from your heart and you are giving with no attachment to the outcome. Helping someone less fortunate than you will give you a wake-up call about how good your life already is. It teaches you to appreciate your blessings. You care about others and want to contribute in a positive way. Just remember it doesn't need to always be a substantial contribution. Little gestures can mean a lot, too. The fact that you are focusing outside yourself to serve others will get you to take your mind off your problems. That result alone makes it all worthwhile.

11. Ask, Ask, Ask for What You Want

You'll probably never have anyone more willing than your leader or mentor to help you achieve your dreams; but they are not mind readers! Learn to ask specifically for what you want, like Markita Andrews did.

Markita Andrews was an eight year old girl whose father had abandoned her and her waitress mother. Both dreamed of traveling around the world. But with their meager income, it seemed unlikely to come true. That all changed at age 13, when Markita read in her Girl Scout magazine that the Scout who sold the most cookies in the country would win an all expense paid trip around the world. Now Markita had a vehicle to realize her dream and she got fired up. Her burning desire to win this trip led her to create a winning action plan.

Dressed in uniform every day after school, she would visit people and ask them to invest in her dream by buying one or two dozen boxes of cookies. Pretty soon, with her drive and determination, Markita had sold 3,256 boxes of Girl Scout cookies. She won the trip around the world and since then has sold more than 42,000 boxes of cookies!

At age 14, she spoke at the international roundtable of the world's top salespeople. Her advice was to ask for the order—ask, ask, ask. True to her motto, she then asked these salespeople to buy her Girl Scout cookies. At that one session, she sold 10,000 boxes of cookies. She's a perfect example of how asking for what you want is key to making your dreams come true.

Ask for whatever you need to make your dream come true. Be clear and specific. Leaders look for people who are eager to make their dreams come true. Imagine your success; picture the person saying yes and helping you. See yourself as fired up and victorious. Let your leader or mentor support you with your dream; it's likely they'll want to help you make it come true. It can get them fired up too.

12. Schedule Action Steps for Your Dream in Your Time/Activity Management System

You may currently be doing something else besides living your dream. That's fairly typical and is no obstacle, as long as you take time to focus and work toward your dream.

Everyone needs to start somewhere. Give attention every day to accomplishing your dream. Use your time/activity management system and schedule in action steps and complete them. That's how you can live your dream, one step at a time, doing whatever it takes. That's what winners do.

13. Attend Seminars Monthly

When you are pursuing your dream, you will find it of great value to attend seminars. There are a wealth of advantages to this. First of all, you will gain valuable information about what it takes to make your dream happen.

Second, you can meet others who are already successful and living their dream who would love to help you with your dream.

Third, associating with others who are fired up and taking action helps you to stay motivated.

Fourth, you can listen to, take notes and maybe even tape record what the speakers are sharing. You can then listen to it over and over again to stay fired up.

14. Counsel With Your Leader or Mentor

Leaders speaking at seminars are experts in their fields. Counseling with your leader or mentor is one of the smartest moves you make to build your business or career. Share your questions and concerns, listen to their advice and take it. They will always have your best interest in mind and will have years of experience. They can help you avoid the mistakes they made. Don't try to build your business or profession alone; ask for help from your leader or mentor.

15. Say Your Affirmations Daily and Make New Ones as Old Ones Come True

Chapter 17 is all about affirmations. You may have discovered they're powerful, they work and are really easy to do. Use them every day, and when you have achieved the goal of a specific affirmation, develop a new one to take its place.

The more you ingrain your success into your subconscious, the further along you can be with your dream. Create your own set of action options for your dream affirmations and move on them. Stoke your fire.

16. Watch Inspirational Videos, Listen to Motivational Audiotapes, and Read Uplifting Books

I personally have benefited greatly from reading positive books. Ask your leader or mentor to recommend some good books to you.

Audiotapes are also a great benefit. They are especially convenient because you can play them while driving, getting ready for work or bed, while you're taking a walk, and while working around the house. Get yourself on a continuing education program of daily tape listening. Listen to at least one of these tapes every day. People who are really moving on have made this a habit.

Some great inspirational movies include: *Field of Dreams, The Boy Who Could Fly, Rudy, Angels in the Outfield, Mr. Holland's Opus, and October Sky.* Perhaps they'll inspire you to move on.

17. Live in the Present Moment

It's easy to focus on the future when you're working on a big dream—and you do need something to aim for—but you will experience greater joy and success when you live in the present moment.

> *The present is the only time in which you can take action. Be open-minded and committed to taking action now and notice how things happen that support you in achieving your dream.*

Keep agreements for the future and visualize your dream as fully realized, while still enjoying today. Remember, *the present is a gift you give to yourself.*

18. Use Music to Inspire, Relax or Energize Yourself

Music can inspire, motivate and soothe. Taste in music is an individual matter; so choose music which supports you best. Some people like soft jazz or classical music for relaxation; while others like country or folk music. Fast music and rock and roll can energize and get you fired up.

Many songwriters feature positive messages which remind you to stay on track. They write songs with meaningful messages which can inspire you to stay focused on your dream and moving on it.

When you attend a seminar where a band is playing, you can often purchase audiotapes of their positive songs. Play them to stay fired up.

19. Use All Your Resources

Chapter 11 outlines your resources in detail. Look over that list periodically and determine whether there are some resources available to you which you may not have taken advantage of yet. Stay on track by using every tool your mentor or leader recommends—*use the system they offer to help you move on.*

20. Have Fun—*Honor the Child Inside Your Heart*

I personally am a big fan of having fun, perhaps because I had a challenging childhood. My husband is one of the best sources for fun ideas, and we schedule it in whenever we can, as long as it doesn't interfere with our goals.

Again, how you like to have fun is up to you. To stay on track, blend your fun with your business activities. For example, at an out of town business function, eat at a local restaurant that looks like a fun place to eat that won't break your budget. If you like cars, go to a car dealership and test drive the car you'd like to own. You'll have fun looking at the cars and meeting other people who like what you like.

Remember that the child inside your heart is a super creative resource for you. You deserve fun and pleasure, as a reward for all the work you do, and to stir up the embers inside of you. Schedule fun into your life, with your priorities in mind. Remember the old adage, "All work and no play makes Jack a dull boy."

21. Exercise in a Way that Supports You

Maybe you're an exercise enthusiast; maybe not. Regardless, as you've probably heard time and time again, exercise is one of the keys to good health and longevity.

Even though I may not feel like it, I exercise regularly and find it gives me more energy for pursuing my dreams. It helps my head to be clear, my body to be sound and my blood to flow. Exercise can sometimes allow you to resolve a problem more easily, because you can put all your effort into taking your walk or whatever exercise you're doing and forget about your worries. Afterwards, you're more relaxed and invigorated and able to tackle the challenges.

Being healthy, which requires eating and exercising in ways that support you, will give you greater strength, both physically and mentally. It will help get you fired up with the flames of energy and life.

22. Laugh Often

Have fun with your business or profession. A great sense of humor will help you to be more flexible in dealing with challenges. Have you ever said, "Someday we'll look back and laugh at this?" Why wait? Laugh at it now! Ask yourself, "In five years, how important will this be?" Probably not very important, right?

Learn not to take yourself too seriously. Enjoy the process as you're doing whatever it takes to reach your goals and dreams. Remember, "Success is a journey, not a destination." Have fun along the way.

Write down some clean jokes and share them while you're talking with others. It'll help "break the ice." So what if you're not yet good at telling jokes. That can be funny in and of itself!

When you're at an out of town business function and have some free time, see if there's a comedy club in the hotel or nearby. Get a few good laughs in and you'll be fired up to attend the next session.

Spencer and I love to laugh. It helps us to get and stay fired up, especially if we start to get negative. It helps us to revitalize and recommit to our journey of personal growth and making dreams come true. Laughing can help you too!

23. Spend Time With Winners

Winner is a subjective term. In sports, it means someone who has competed and triumphed. A winner in life is someone with an optimistic outlook who has a great attitude about life and gets things done. A winner is joyful and open to the opportunity to learn, stretch, and grow. A winner looks for the best in others, rather than criticizing or complaining— they're goodfinders. A real winner has occasional setbacks, but when they fall down, they pick themselves up, dust themselves off and keep going, always focused on their goal.

If you had the choice of associating with a negative- thinking person or a winner, wouldn't you rather spend the day with a winner? Which one would encourage you and inspire you to move forward? Which one would show appreciation for you and your victories and give you honest feedback? Think about these questions when you decide who to share your dream with, or even who to spend your free time with. Negative thinking people bring others down; so stay away from them as much as possible. Hang around with winners instead. Keep going up and up, like a hot air balloon, toward your dreams and goals.

24. Do Random Acts of Kindness

In 1983 a California artist decided she would do unexpected favors for strangers, in an effort to make the world a better place. Her actions caught on and the concept of *Random Acts of Kindness* resulted in a bestselling book of the same name, published by the editors of Conari Press.

Most of the gestures described in that book are small, simple acts of kindness, yet they make a large difference in the lives of those they touch. Why? As the book says, *"At the foundation of every act of kindness is a simple and compassionate connection between strangers, who, for a moment, aren't strangers anymore....Kindness, it seems, has the capacity to return us to the very core of our humanity."*

Practicing acts of kindness is a wonderful way to quickly get fired up about who you are as a person. Something as seemingly inconsequential as paying a stranger's toll at the highway tollbooth, or putting money in someone's parking meter, or smiling at the checkout person at the grocery store can mean a great deal to those people. And who knows, you just might meet a great friend in the process!

I had a sweet experience with this when a group of us were focusing on kindness as a theme one week. I was grocery shopping and at the checkout counter, when I started chatting with the woman in front of me. She was obviously from another country and was getting accustomed to our prices. I commented on how I loved chocolate, as there was a cookbook for sale at the checkout counter with a chocolate cake on the cover. She said she loved making desserts and experimenting with new recipes, but that cookbook was not in her week's budget. As her groceries were being bagged, I bought her the cookbook. To avoid any embarrassment that she might have felt, I quickly added, "It's Kindness Week" and told her that I would like her to have the cookbook. She rewarded me with a great big smile and a simple thank you. Little things can mean a lot. Giving, especially when it's expected, is such fun and so heartwarming. Try it and find out for yourself. You'll be fired up too!

25. Have Faith That You'll Succeed

Faith is belief in things unseen. And you only need to have a little of it to start making your dreams come true. That small seed of faith will cause you to start believing that you can do it.

As you make progress toward your dreams, you'll become more inspired to keep going—and your dreams will grow.

Your vision of how your life can be comes from faith. This then leads to a greater understanding of why you are here, and what you are to be doing with your life.

Faith is essential for your true happiness, joy and success—which are the results of fulfilling your purpose in life.

As the old saying goes, "Keep the faith." Go forward in faith and help others in their quest to achieve their dreams—in keeping with your purpose—and you can achieve yours.

26. Celebrate Success and Bring Joy to Others

In the Walt Disney movie, *Pollyanna,* the main character is a little girl who was orphaned and sent to live with her "crusty" old aunt. In spite of her harsh surroundings and the strict treatment she receives, Pollyanna maintains a sweet, upbeat disposition and brings joy to the people in her community.

One particularly poignant example of Pollyanna's engaging nature occurred when she visited an elderly woman and her daughter. The older woman was a negative-thinking person, and a rather loud, complaining one at that. She stayed in bed all day, whining and moaning and trying to make everyone else's life miserable, too. Pollyanna visited her, and magically transformed the woman's outlook. She took the crystal prisms that were attached to her lamps, and hung them in the sunlit window so that tiny rainbows sparkled throughout the room.

The effect was enchanting, and the old woman was delighted with the results. She settled down, stopped whining and really enjoyed the effect. To Pollyanna, the whole thing was minor and fun; to the woman, it was a very big deal.

That's what I mean when I say spread joy to others. Your actions may be very small and simple, but they can uplift and contribute to someone else's healing process as well as get you and others fired up. One way to give happiness is to celebrate success. Every time you have a win, share it with someone who cares about you and will be happy for you.

Also celebrate with your business associates and your family when they have a victory. Go out to breakfast, lunch or dinner or have a cupcake together (with a candle, of course). Do something inexpensive, fun and spontaneous. Celebrate all of life's big and little special moments along the way, blending it with your business or profession as much as you can. It will make every day worthwhile for you and others you care about.

Spreading happiness is a form of service. Joy is contagious. The more you share it with others, the more joyful you feel yourself. It's a terrific win-win experience that helps keep your fire burning.

27. Share the Dream

Many people think about their dreams and would like them to come true. But typically, they either don't believe they can do it or don't know what to do to make it happen. That's where you come in. You can help them bridge the gap between their current situation and their dream of how they'd like to live—that is, if they're serious about their future. You can be an encourager.

Talk to others about their dreams. You could ask, "What would you do if you had all the time and money in the world?" Listen to them and encourage them to describe their dreams to you. Believe in them and their ability to live their dreams. Tell them they can do it. Cheer them on. Help them to get fired up about what could happen for them.

This exchange may lead to creating a new friend. Realize your ability to take an interest in others and get them fired up. Your gifts of enthusiasm and compassion are priceless. You can build friendships, as well as your business or profession, using your unique gifts. Always share the dream to reach someone's heart. That's where the fire starts to burn and that's where their dreams live. *When you inspire others to dream, you'll dream bigger yourself!*

Chapter 23

You Can Make A Difference In The World

Sharing Your Fire's Warmth with Others

"I expect to pass through life but once. If, therefore, there be any kindness I can show, or any good thing I can do let me do it now...as I will not pass this way again."
William Penn

Are You Fired Up?

You're using the tools in this book and you're moving forward in a positive way. You're motivated, excited and starting to live your dreams, or at least you're moving in that direction. Now what?

Are You Fired Up? Principle #32—*Make a Difference!*

You have an opportunity to spread hope. Go out and plant "dream seeds" and keep the dream alive for as many people as you can. Get them fired up and moving on. How about lifting others into a more positive experience, putting smiles on their faces and sharing your blessings and enthusiasm? "How do I do that?" you may ask. It's simple. When you are fired up you positively influence the lives of those around you. In many cases, your excitement helps to uplift others and shakes them out of their negativity.

What causes would you like to support more fully? Are you a medical doctor who wants to donate your services, in your country or abroad, to the needy? Do you have a charity you're particularly fond of that you would like to contribute more money to? Perhaps something like the missions Mother Teresa set up during her lifetime or an organization that is committed to the cure and elimination of a particular disease? This is a very personal decision. There are many worthy causes in need of support.

Making a difference doesn't have to be a big deal, either. It can be simple and easy, as it often is. You can make a difference every day. Perhaps you just bought a new puppy and, while on a walk, you let little children pet it and giggle.

Your favorite baseball team just won and you whistle as you walk down the street, causing others to smile. You feel happy about your experiences that day and smile at the grocery clerk, and she feels encouraged. You greet a weary telephone caller with a cheerful "Hello, I'm glad you called," and they feel valued.

You extend a little kindness to an elderly neighbor by carrying their bags to the door or sweeping their sidewalk—they know somebody cares. You feed the birds and they reward you by chirping and visiting daily. You help others take action on their dreams and they get fired up. Or perhaps you just take two minutes to speak to a stranger when no one else has and they appreciate your attention.

All of these are examples of being fired up and touching the lives of others. In your own special way, you can ignite the flames of other people and make a difference in their lives—many times without even realizing it!

Maria Is Making a Difference

Growing up in a communist country was not easy for Maria. Both her Bulgarian parents worked hard, and her father's strict disciplinary approach taught her to be strong.

At age 14, Maria decided to leave home and go to an English-speaking school. It was there that her dream of being a doctor was born. Throughout the next several years, she studied and worked with dedication and fervor. She eventually became a respected physician with a speciality in neurology, and was chosen to work in the University Hospital. But in 1993 she fell in love with an American and moved to the United States to share his vision.

Happily married, she never gave up her longing for practicing medicine. After passing the American medical exams, she expected to resume life as a doctor. Months of interviewing taught her how difficult it was for foreign doctors to work in the U.S. She knew the only way for her to succeed was to get a residency at one of the hospitals in the Boston area. She interviewed with hospitals, made phone calls, observed medical procedures and made professional contacts wherever possible. Maria got fired up. She took consistent action on her dream and did everything she could to make it come true.

Just two months later, she heard that she had not been chosen for any of the residencies for which she had applied. Undaunted, she continued to take action. That very same day, while observing at a Boston hospital, she asked an American co-worker to put in a good word for her with the hiring physician there. He did and, later that day, after she had spoken extensively with that physician, she was hired! She triumphed over dozens of other physicians, American and foreign, for the one available residency. She had made her dream come true!

Now she lights up the lives of those she works with and shares her delight at being able to live her dream fully. She is still fired up and not only makes a big difference in the lives of the patients that she helps heal, but also in the lives of her medical colleagues. They feel the warmth of her fire, enthusiasm, and dedication. It also reminds them why they originally decided to become doctors. Maria had helped them learn to appreciate why they do what they do. This has re-ignited their internal flames.

Making a Difference in Mississippi

Osceola McCarthy worked most of her life in the U.S. as an uneducated black washerwoman in Hattiesburg, Mississippi. Even when washing machines became popular, she preferred to wash clothing by hand in a boiling pot to give the highest quality wash. Amazingly, she charged only 50¢ a bundle, which rose to $10 a bundle in later years.

With no children of her own, Osceola had the dream of helping out other African Americans in the area. In 1995 she donated her whole life savings of $150,000 to the University of Southern Mississippi for scholarships for black college students. "I want them to have an education" she says, "I had to work hard all my life. They can have the chance that I didn't have."

Osceola's generosity has astonished her community; so much so that matching funds have been raised by area businesses. Equally common is the question she receives so often: "Why didn't you spend the money on yourself?" She answers with a big, loving smile, "I *am* spending it on myself." Osceola is fired up and making a difference in the lives of others. Every graduating student sets her fire ablaze.

Making a Difference Through Loving Support

At a National Speaker's Association Convention, someone told a story about the Special Olympics in Seattle a few years ago. Nine youngsters, all either physically or mentally challenged, gathered at the start of the 100-yard dash. When the gun sounded, they took off, with enthusiasm for winning the race; that is, all except for one boy, who tripped on the asphalt, tumbled a few times and burst into tears. The other contestants heard him cry. One by one, they all halted, paused and went back to the distraught boy. One girl with Down's syndrome bent over him, gave him a kiss on his cheek and said, "This will make it better." All nine contestants linked arms and walked together over the finish line. They got a standing ovation and the cheering lasted for ten minutes. The crowd was fired up and touched by the loving support these youngsters demonstrated for each other.

What Are The Keys to Making a Difference in the World?

In each of these cases, people got fired up about their dream, and in some way reached out and made a difference in the lives of others. Making a difference in the world is not difficult at all. You do it far more often than you realize.

In most examples of making a difference in the world:

- ◆ Action is taken, either inwardly or outwardly.
- ◆ This action contributes in a positive way to someone or something often by inspiring, supporting their healing process, helping or creating.
- ◆ Enthusiasm is "in the air." People are fired up!

The interesting thing about touching others while you're fired up is that you often do it without even being consciously aware of it. This next story illustrates the point.

A Little Boy Lights Up Others

My husband and I were sitting in a pancake restaurant on a rainy Saturday. Many people were allowing the weather to dampen their moods; the atmosphere was quiet and glum. All of a sudden, a very young boy sauntered into the restaurant with his parents. After they were seated, he excitedly ran up and down the aisles, giggling all the way.

He was simply fired up about life, eating pancakes and being with his parents. His father chased him, laughing and having fun with his exuberant son.

Pretty soon almost everyone in the restaurant began smiling. Several people chuckled, lightened by the child's joy. He lit up the whole restaurant, just by being himself, and enjoying the experience. He made a positive difference that day and each laugh stirred the sparks inside the other people.

The same thing is true of you when you share your enthusiasm, happiness and good nature. This results from your fired up attitude about your life. You're doing what you love, or working towards it, and making your dreams come true.

A Few Tips to Remember

When you are fired up about your dreams, your enthusiasm and energy can be enormous. When you value other people and truly want to make a difference in their lives, while you're living your dream or are moving in that direction, here are a few tips that can help.

Tip #1—*Share From Your Heart*

When you are fired up and the flame inside you burns brightly, *share with others authentically from your heart.* When you are talking about your dream and how you made it come true, be sure to mention the challenges along the way and how you overcame them. Let them know what kind of effort and energy you put into your dream, so they can realize that it's possible for them, too. Be humble—understand and share that everything you have achieved has been with lots of help from other people.

Communicate that you are appreciative of the help others have given you by believing in you and supporting you every step of the way. Nobody can be successful alone. Let others know how grateful you are for all the wonderful gifts in your life. Give others hope that they can do it, too.

Tip #2—*Ask Questions and Listen*

When you're reaching out and sharing with others, be sure to ask them what dreams they have and how they feel about them. Ask them to describe what they love to do, and what they have always hoped they could accomplish. Encourage them to keep talking while, most of all, listening carefully to what they have to say.

Remember how, in the beginning of the book, you did the listening exercise with another person? The most important guideline of that activity was to be quiet and not interrupt the other person. Let them have all the time they need to share about their dreams. They're likely to appreciate your caring attention.

You'll be able to watch the sparks igniting inside of them and their faces becoming animated. They will get fired up right in front of you. Listening is one of the most caring things you can do for someone. Make it a regular part of your interactions with others. They'll like being with you.

Tip #3—*Be Unattached to the Outcome*

Remember—*be unattached to the outcome of your sharing or making a difference.* Service, by its very nature, means contributing to the welfare of others, assisting them in some way, *without expecting anything in return.* The best kind of service is done lovingly from the heart, with the intention of doing so for the benefit of all concerned.

Don't measure your self-worth based on the outcome of your intentions with others. Remember, other people's behavior is always about themselves. Even though you may want to help someone, they may not want help, for whatever reason. Let them pursue their dreams or not, the way they choose. Let go of any fear or concern that they do things your way. They may need to experience some more challenges before they're motivated enough to get out of their comfort zone and do something to make a difference in their lives.

Every year, there's a TV show called *Party for the Planet,* which honors young people from around the country who do special projects to improve the environment. Schools, clubs, and organizations with young people of all ages, from all walks of life, enter and participate in the competition. The best ones are showcased in a national celebration on television.

Each of these groups does their best and works hard to make a difference in the earth itself. Sometimes their results don't turn out the way they expected. Some projects span over years. And there are people who have worked very hard who don't get the national media attention that the winners get. That doesn't mean their work is any less valuable; it's just that someone else's project was noticed and got chosen. If these youngsters were to stop doing their projects because of that, it would show that their hearts were not in it.

When you serve, let go of any attachment to a specific outcome. Do your personal best; that's the most you can do! Remember—the journey is the success; the outcome is the reward.

Tip #4—*Give Them Freedom to Have Their Own Dreams*
You're fired up, living your dream (or in the process of doing so), and taking advantage of all that is available to you. Your life is going better than it ever has and you are developing tremendous success and happiness. So who would be better than you to help other people with their dreams? Share your excitement, and by all means, listen and engage them in positive, upbeat activities like dreambuilding.

But give others *their* freedom. Don't try to change or "fix" them or have them live their lives your way. Focus on helping others make *their* dreams come true, big or small, and yours will come true.

Respect that each person has their own personal history, making them unique. They learn in different ways and do things in their own time. Let them. Give them the space they need. Support and encourage them; offer suggestions and help if they want it, but let *them* do it. Did you ever try something new with your parents when you were a kid—like riding a bike or building a model? It was just something you had to experience to get the satisfaction of doing it.

Watching someone else do it wasn't enough. So, you did it yourself, the best way you knew how. That's how you learned and achieved. And that's how others learn, too. As Dale Carnegie once said, *"A man convinced against his will is of the same opinion still."* Share what you have with others—set a good example and let them learn and grow by doing it by themselves.

In my experience as a trainer, it has been enormously gratifying to watch people get fired up and take off in pursuit of their dreams. Most have been successful, and some are still working on it. But out of all the successes, not one has ever done it exactly the same way as the others. Each individual's personal history and unique approach to life has colored and impacted everything about their dream. These factors made their dream real and personal for them. I have loved watching and learning, listening and experiencing the rich diversity of the human heart—it can teach us all so much.

Tip #5—*Share Your Love*

The best way to make a difference in the lives of others is to—*sincerely share your love for others.* Authentically share from your heart the caring or empathy you have for others. This means exhibiting kindness, going the extra mile and giving others the benefit of the doubt. It means letting the past go and living in the present. It means stepping forward and doing what needs to be done to help another human being. Loving means laughing and experiencing joy and sharing the interaction. It means reaching out and touching others genuinely in friendship and goodwill. It means sharing your ideas with the attitude that they can really make a difference in that person's life.

Celebrate other people's successes, no matter how small. Encourage them when they face disappointments. Remind them of their talents and greatness. Continually help them to keep their flame alive. Help them stoke the embers if they go out. Help them ignite their dreams and stay fired up.

The "Give Kids The World" Foundation

One of the many programs designed to help terminally ill children enjoy their last few months of life is "Give Kids the World" Henri Landwirth founded this international non-profit foundation in 1986 to bring sick children and their families to DisneyWorld. This program pays expenses for the sick children and their families, including round trip airfare from over forty countries outside the U.S.

In 1989 Henri opened "Kids Village" near DisneyWorld in Kissimmee, Florida, which provides housing for 4,000 families on 35 acres of land. The village includes a castle and carousel, a lake with live fish, a welcome center, the Gingerbread House dining area and 56 villas. A doctor is always on call to tend to the terminally ill children while they are visiting.

The whole purpose of the foundation is to help bring joy into the lives of these children and their families. Happily, they regularly achieve this goal. "The happiest six days of my child's life" was how one parent described their visit. Henri Landwirth was recently honored as one of the twelve most caring people in America. As his life so clearly demonstrates, one person can indeed make a difference. As Winston Churchill once said, *"We make a living by what we get. We make a life by what we give."*

Always Remember This

Inside you is the fire of life. That fire is your passion, your life purpose, your mission, and your fulfillment. It burns brightly inside you and ignites when you're doing whatever it takes to do what you love and live your dreams. It re-ignites every time you share the dream with others and make a positive difference in their lives. When you're fired up and "on fire" for your dream, your fire warms others, ignites their flames, and creates enthusiasm and joy.

You *can* overcome any obstacle, meet any challenge and win. You were born with greatness inside you. The time to start working towards living the life you dream of and sharing the dream with others is now. Ignite the flame inside, stay fired up, and keep moving on your dreams. Live your life with joy and success. Be fired up. It's not just a state of temporary excitement—*it's a way of life that can change the world.*

Now Take These *Are You Fired Up?* Action Steps

- ◆ Actively think about who you'd like to serve and share the dream with. Begin making a difference in the world with the people in your life.
- ◆ Consider what charities or non-profit groups you admire and whose work you would like to support. Ask yourself, "What could I do to help these causes once I'm financially able?" Put something to represent that dream on your dream list and dream collage.
- ◆ Once you have achieved a dream, it's time for your next dream. Use the tools of this book as you dream bigger and get fired up all over again. Live your life with joy and success. Keep the fire alive inside you and share your caring and enthusiasm with others, making a difference every day.

The *Are You Fired Up?* Creed

Inside me is the fire of life. That fire is my passion, my life purpose, my mission and fulfillment. It burns brightly as I pursue my dreams. I get fired up by regularly scheduling what I love to do. I am clear about what I want and I use my vivid imagination. I regularly visualize my dreams as fully realized and I create dream collages to stoke my fire. As a fired up person, I act "as if" I am already living my dream. I dreambuild, connect with the right people and ask for what I want. I am open to receive the wisdom and assistance of others who are where I want to be and I express my appreciation for their help. I thank God for giving me my dreams and the ability to make them come true. As a fired up person, I use all the career or business-building tools my leader or mentor recommends, take care of my health, use my time wisely, manage my money effectively and get out of debt. I stay fired up by laughing often and watching inspirational movies and having fun in everything I do. I read from a positive book and listen to positive tapes every day. I attend seminars and other business related activities every month. As a fired up person, I create affirmations for my dreams and support them with action options. I take action on my dream every day. I overcome all obstacles and nothing keeps me from achieving my dreams. As a fired up person, I invite the child locked inside my heart to come out and play and share their creativity and enthusiasm with me. As a fired up person, I keep going, no matter what, doing whatever it takes. I pursue my dreams with passion, persistence and a positive vision of the outcome. I associate with winners regularly and share the dream with others. I use every experience as an opportunity to learn and grow. By working toward doing what I love and staying fired up, I make a positive difference in the world each day. I share my heart and gifts with the world.

Yes—*I Am Fired Up!*

© 2000, Anne Whiting

About the Author

Anne Whiting is a speaker, trainer and author. In 1983 she founded her own advertising and training agency, and continues on as president and creative director. Her trademark qualities are her genuine enthusiasm and an ability to get people fired up.

Anne began her professional career as an educator, and is still actively involved with youth through organizations like Project Safeguard and the YMCA. A keynote motivational speaker and trainer for general adult audiences, associations, conventions, organizations, and corporations, she is also a member of the National Speaker's Association.

Anne lives with her husband Spencer and their two cats, and loves to sail, travel, write, dance, and entertain. Her passion is to help people to be more successful in life and to live their dreams.